One Hundred Poems of
CHOKHA MELA

Bilingual Edition

Translated & Introduced by

CHANDRAKANT KALURAM MHATRE

Sitaram Mhatre Foundation
Navi Mumbai
www.sitarammhatre.foundation

One Hundred Poems of Chokha Mela: Bilingual Edition

Translated & Introduced by
Chandrakant Kaluram Mhatre

Published by
SITARAM MHATRE FOUNDATION
Registered Office
Sitaram Smaran, 896, Sector 19B,
Koparkhairane, Navi Mumbai 400709
Email: info@sitarammhatre.foundation
www.sitarammhatre.foundation

First Edition December 2023
ISBN (Paperback) 978-81-960911-7-0

Printed at
Createspace
Middletown, DE, USA

Cover, Typesetting & Book Design
Chandrakant Kaluram Mhatre

To
my grandfather,
Late Sitaram G. Mhatre,
for him forgiveness came so naturally,
even when it was not
the least deserved
by its recipient

CONTENTS

ACKNOWLEDGMENTS

Forever
in loving debt of
Chandrakala, Aruna, Nancy & Grishma,
for their tireless hard work made this happen
– yet once again!

FOREWORD

With the introduction of *One Hundred Poems of Chokha Mela* as a prescribed text for "Indian Literature in Translation" course of M.A. (Honours) in English & M.A. (Honours with Research) in English programmes of the University of Mumbai, a need was felt for the bilingual edition of the book to facilitate side-by-side exploration of the source and target texts. Apart from proving critical for better understanding and appreciation of Sant Chokha Mela's poems, the idea of such an edition appealed to me a great deal as it could enable the students and the scholars to understand and assess my translation process. To make this possible, the source poem and its translation are given on the same page next to each other in this edition. However, instead of the traditional layout of the abhang, this edition presents these poems in the form that they are composed in, viz. four-line or two-line stanzas. Q: Why? A: To fully appreciate any poem, one must be able to perceive it in the form it was conceived (We must bear in mind that the traditional layout was adopted as the practical means to minimize the number of pages, and no other reason). For long, the abhang form has been so blatantly mangled by the translators of bhakti poetry as if it were their birthright. I sincerely hope that, in their translations, the coming generations of translators will pay the due respect to the form of these exquisitely beautiful lyrics.

I take this opportunity to congratulate the University of Mumbai's Dept. of English & its HOD, Dr. Rajesh Karankal for daring to be so inclusive as to become perhaps the very first Dept. of English in India to include Chokha Mela in its curriculum. Chokhoba has waited for seven centuries at the doorsteps and it's high time that more and more universities become equally inclusive in these divided times.

Navi Mumbai — Chandrakant Kaluram Mhatre
December 2023

INTRODUCTION

History of discrimination among human beings on one basis or other is as old as the history of humankind itself. In fact, one dares to state that the discrimination in one form or other has been the foundation of human civilization in all places and in all times. What is assuring in this deeply murky history is the equally resonating fact that the history of rebellions against all kinds of discrimination is as old as the origin of discrimination itself. At some points in history, these rebellions have been limited to individuals; at other times, entire societies have stood up in rebellion against the oppressions of discrimination. Some of these rebellions were brutally crushed using monstrous force, while a good number of rebellions have been so successful that discriminating powers were wiped out of the face of the earth. One such rebellion took place in Maharashtra in the thirteenth century and went on for centuries to come. It was one of the most successful rebellions ever and that too without using violence at all - even verbal violence was unthinkable to these rebels! They did not believe in doing away with the practitioners of discrimination - instead, they successfully attempted to do away with the mentality that establishes and encourages discrimination in the name of caste /class /creed /colour /gender. They were all followers of Varkari Sampraday, a unique sect within Hinduism founded by Sant Dnayndev and Sant Namdev in the last decade of the thirteenth century. So successful was this rebellion of the Varkaris against discrimination that the most impactful voice against such oppression came from a person belonging to one of the most downtrodden communities of that time: Chokha Mela!

He was born in the Mahar community which lay at the bottom of the caste hierarchy prevalent in the contemporary society. Of course, he was not to have any education even in the remotest sense of the word. Yet, such was the influence of the two founding fathers and other saints of the Varkari Sect that Chokha Mela could compose poetry of the highest order. Poetry that has stood the test of time for last seven hundred years and has become the finest example of the expression of human angst caused by the oppressive societal norms. Each poem by Chokha Mela, or Chokhoba as he was fondly called by his peers, stands testimony to the inhuman treatment that was meted out to large sections of society in the name of religion. Each of his poems is a cry of the bereaved soul that has been deprived of its humanness itself. Each of the poem is a powerful statement against the repression that a handful carried out against the masses. Such is the intensity of these poems that their reader feels the very angst that the Poet must have undergone. Such is the grip that these poems take over the reader's mind that one feels their guts being wrenched, remembering the agony of the Poet's expressions long after the poems have been read and the book kept aside.

What gives Chokhoba's poems such a power over their readers? In their very basic form, they are 'poems of protest' and one has to accept that any protest literature has the limitations of contemporaneity. Yesterday's intense protest poem may appear entirely lifeless today. Yesteryear's immensely moving protest poem may come across as mundane altogether today. But this certainly is not the case with Chokhoba's poems which were mostly composed in the first decades of the fourteenth century, making them exactly seven hundred years old. These centuries, however, have not succeeded in diminishing the power of the poems even by a degree. In fact, given our times' essential belief in the human rights of every individual, these poems gain much more power to move than they had earlier. How has Chokhoba succeeded in overcoming the basic limitation of protest literature then? Answers to this fundamental question will vary from reader to reader, but for me what matters the most is the fact that Chokha Mela did not use his poems as a means of protest but self-expression. And it is this genuine expression of his anguished heart that has given his poems the timelessness that they have been enjoying from the times even before the birth of Geoffrey Chaucer.

What kind of self-expression does one come across in Chokha Mela's poems? The entire spectrum of human feelings, doubts, epiphanies, predicaments and realizations of the highest order are the stuff that these poems are made of. What is significant is that all these expressions in these poems are easily the experiences of the common-most human being, the Poet's sainthood does not raise its spectre between him and his reader. On every word of these poems, the reader gets the feeling that what is being expressed is exactly their own heart's cry - no matter at which place and in which times they are born! Chokhoba's expression becomes the expression of each of his reader, overcoming all the barriers of social, cultural, historical and geographical restrains. This is what has enabled his poems to resound in every age and every place. They have been communicating with their readers (erstwhile listeners, for his poems were mainly sung/recited) the essential human predicament - having to choose between one's lot and one's aspirations!

What was it that Chokha Mela aspired for? What was it with his aspirations that went against his predestined 'lot'? To understand this, we will have to traverse seven hundred years back to the thirteenth century. There are no convincing records about Chokha Mela's birth year or birth place, but we know for sure that he was a contemporary of Sant Dnyandev and Sant Namdev. He has even described the occasion of Dnyandev's 'Samadhi Eternal'[1] in one of his poems, accurately recording the date of that momentous event in the history of Varkari Sect. Also, his poems elaborating upon his discipleship of Sant Namdev give us a fair idea about his times. However, the best source to determine Chokhoba's times is the biographical poems of Namdev himself who has recorded important events in the lives of all his contemporary saints with historical accuracy. All these literary evidences squarely place Chokhoba in the final decades of the thirteenth century and the initial decades of the fourteenth century. His place of birth though remains a bone of contention. What we know for sure is that he spent a considerable part of his life in Pandharpur[2] - of course far away from the main settlement owing to his caste.

Chokha Mela was born in the Mahar community which was considered to be the 'untouchables' by the then so-called higher castes owing to the menial work that was assigned to them. The Mahars were to maintain the cleanliness and the hygiene in the society mainly by disposing off the carcasses of dead animals including the cattle. And it was this society-assigned work of theirs on the basis of which the same society considered them as source of pollution and avoided even their shadows, let alone their touch. They were denied every single human right that we uphold so religiously today. There was no education for them, no possibility of changing their profession and no any other means of livelihood like land. Basically, they were dispossessed of their human status itself and had to survive begging for the leftovers of the higher caste people for this was how they were paid for all their back-breaking scavenging work. Even when these stale leftovers were given to them, they were dropped into their bamboo baskets from such a distance to avoid the pollution that would cause by an accidental touch! In case of such a calamity of having polluted by the touch of such a person, the higher castes would immediately resort to ablution to wash off the effects of that pollution.

Such was the 'lot' of Chokha Mela. So, when he arrived in Pandharpur with his wife Soyara somewhere in the 1280-90

CE, he had no option but to erect a hut for themselves on the opposite bank of River Bhima on whose bank the main settlement and the Vitthal temple was situated. Chokha had reached Pandharpur[2] having heard about the revolution that the Varkaris were trying to bring in the contemporary society by advocating complete annihilation of all kinds of discrimination. While all his brethren were happy with their lot, Chokha aspired for something better, something nobler than mere sense-perception existence that he has described in his poems as:

My own community
Have to eat impious
Liquor and meat
Their meals comprise

or

Sycophants, thieves, womanizers
Corrupt through and through
Debased existence for eternity
Is their destiny.

What sets Chokha apart from this 'debased existence' is his desire to rise above his lot. He desired for a better life - not in the material sense of that much-maligned phrase but something far superior than that. He did not desire for better food, better house or better clothing, instead he desired for the human dignity which was not to be associated with his caste at all. It was almost equal to asking for a moon! But that was what Chokha desired for - to be treated as an equal, which gets an expression in his poems thus:

To avoid my touch
No one seats near me
Chokha says such is
Life mine

or

No one accepts me
In their company
"Get lost from here"
Says one and all

and

Outcaste that we are
What rights we have?
Everyone shoos us
Far away.

Throughout his poems, Chokha keeps asking questions about his rights, or rather their absence. This awareness of one's rights is something that shapes much of his character. He is so assured of his own worth as a poet, as a devotee of the Lord Vitthal that his low caste status does not fill him with the kind of diffidence that plagues almost anyone who has been subjugated to such kind of extreme repression as the Mahar community. This psychological strength is the most valuable gift that Chokha received from his Varkari mentors. This strength is what enabled him to question all the injustices heaped upon him in the name of untouchability and pollution:

Then how can one be pure
And the other impure
If the origin of pollution
Is our bodies?

and

Pollution of the Five
Within one body
Then pure in the world
How can be any?

The very fact that a member of the lowest caste could question the hegemony of the predominant classes signifies a lot about the extent of the revolution that the Varkaris had set in motion. That such poems were not and could not be suppressed and destroyed speaks volume about the eminence that Chokha Mela had earned among these circles. One gets a distinct idea of Chokha's eminence when one comes across him questioning the sacrosanct scriptures itself in his poems:

Pollution for Vedas
Pollution for Shastras
Puranas are filled with
Demeaning pollution.

However, all was this hunky-dory only till Chokha was among his Varkari companions. The moment he would step out of that enlightened circle, he would have to face the atrocities at the hands of the higher echelons of the society, especially the Brahmins. How could a Mahar rise to the status of sainthood? How could someone, who is to be but trampled upon at every instance, be allowed to be revered by others socially superior to him. That was a challenge to the very existence of the caste hierarchy. Blinded by this rage and the pathetic belief in their own superiority, the Brahmins of Pandharpur began to persecute Chokha and his entire family every which way possible. This persecution was not only limited to verbal humiliation but went even beyond physical assaults: they accused Chokha of stealing from the Vitthal temple. One of the most well-known of Chokhoba's poems speaks of this incident:

Rush forth, O Vithu, do not walk so slow
The priests beat me up, whatever my crime

"How has Vithoba's garland reached your neck?"
They curse me, call me Mahar, "The Lord's been defiled"

Chokhoba's stay in Pandhari had become almost impossible but his love for his deity Vitthal and his Guru Namdev was so great that he could never think of leaving Pandhari and faced all these atrocities with immense courage. At times, such cruel was the treatment given to Chokhoba that his heart was filled with doubts regarding his own beliefs, even his faith. These excruciating moments have got such an expression in his poems that one feels the strongest tug possible at the heart while reading them - making one wonder how would have this man undergone with all these miseries and sorrows and yet retain his faith!

Chokhoba's faith is indeed unique. He loved the deity - even at the risk of his dear life - which he was not even able to see, for he was not ever allowed to enter the temple of Lord Vitthal. All he could reach was up to the door of the temple, waiting outside with folded hands to be allowed inside. This is the most poignant image in all of Chokha's poems:

Choked up Chokha
Stands at His door
Entreating the Lord
With folded hands.

It almost takes form of a powerful symbol when one reads his poems in a succession with this image hitting one constantly, appearing in so many different forms and dimensions:

Not speak any further
That alone would be wise
Will become a rock
Lying at Your door

or

Give me place
At Your door
This is all, O Lord
I ask of You

and

At His door Chokha Mela
Beholds Vitthal with own eyes.

In the end, however, the Brahmins succeeded in making Chokha leave Pandharpur as he was among the Mahars who were made to work on the construction of town-wall at a nearby place called Mangalavedha. In many decades, for the first time Chokha was separated from his beloved Lord and the poems that he composed during his stay there are distinctly poignant:

My end is nigh
It seems to me
What was destined
Has happened

From birth, dependent
Have been servant Yours
Now in the end
I lie far away.

When one reads these poems knowing the historical fact that Chokha could never return to Pandahrpur from Mangalvedha, they begin to signify on a different level altogether. During the construction of the town-wall, a portion of it collapsed, killing a number of Mahar labourers under it - Chokha being one of them. Namdev brought his bones back to Pandharpur and built his Samadhi (final resting place) right in front of the Vitthal temple's main entrance. Today, anyone who visits the Vitthal temple at Pandharpur, first pays their obeisance to Chokhoba and then only enters the temple to see the Lord. For others this Samadhi might stand for many other things, for me it stands as an emblem of the victory of the indomitable human aspirations over Fate.

I find Chokhoba's poems extremely tragic in tone and equally cathartic in function. No doubt they are very significant as social documents, recording the protest against caste discrimination. But fortunately, they transcend this utility and enter the realm of pure art that makes human life much more meaningful. It is high time that we stop looking at this poet as a mere social documenter and begin to appreciate and assess him as a poet-artist of the highest order.

Navi Mumbai Chandrakant Kaluram Mhatre
May 2015

NOTES:

1 Yogis of highest order would bring their life to completion by absorbing themselves into the deepest possible meditation, attaining absolute unison with the Creation, while seated in a sealed underground chamber.

2 Pandharpur, also known as Pandhari, is a town in Solapur district of Maharashtra, that houses the temple of Lord Vitthal, also known as Pandurang, the Supreme deity of the Varkari Sect.

ꕥꕥꕥ || 1 || ꕥꕥꕥ

Sugarcane misshapen, but the sap is not
Why be charmed with mere appearance?

Bow misshapen, but the arrow is not
Why be charmed with mere appearance?

River misshapen, but the water is not
Why be charmed with mere appearance?

Chokha misshapen, but the faith is not
Why be charmed with mere appearance

ऊस डोंगा परी रस नोहे डोंगा ।
काय भुललासी वरलीया रंगा ॥१॥

कमान डोंगी परी तीर नोहे डोंगा ।
काय भुललासी वरलीया रंगा ॥२॥

नदी डोंगी पर जळ नोहे डोंगे ।
काय भुललासी वरलीया रंगा ॥३॥

चोखा डोंगा परी भाव नोहे डोंगा ।
काय भुललासी वरलीया रंगा ॥४॥

ꟹꟹꟹ || **2** || ꟹꟹꟹ

I saw, I saw The Lord of yogis Rukmadevi's Spouse From Pandhari	देखिला देखिला योगियांचा रावो । रुक्मादेवीनाहो पंढरीचा ॥१॥
Owing to Pundalik[1] For twenty-eight eons Has assumed cherub-form On the banks of Bhima	पुंडलिकासाठी युगे अठ्ठावीस । धरोनि बाळवेष भीमातटी ॥२॥
Cows and calves Together with Vaishnavs Dance the cowherds For the love of Vitthal	गाई गोपाळ वत्से वैष्णवांचा मेळ । नाचत गोपाळ विठ्ठल छंदे ॥३॥
Chokha Mela there Bows to touch feet Lies prostrate At His door	चोखामेळा तेथे वंदितो चरण । घाली लोटांगण महाद्वारी ॥४॥

1 The legend says that it was for Pundalik that Lord Krishna arrived in Pandhari and assumed the form of Lord Vitthal. Thus, Pundalik is accorded the honour of being the originator of the cult of Lord Vitthal.

ଔଔଔ || 3 || ഋഋഋ

Hearing of the ears Smelling of the nose Tasting of the tongue Vitthal mine	श्रवणाचे श्रवण घ्राणाचे जे घ्राण । रसने गोडपण विठ्ठल माझा ॥१॥
Makes tongue speak Makes eyes see Makes organs perform Vitthal mine	वाचा जेणे उठी डोळा जेणे भेटी । इंद्रियांची राहाटी विठ्ठल माझा ॥२॥
Makes breath move Keeps mind restrained Distinct from nothingness Vitthal mine	प्राण जेणे चळे मन तेणे वोळे । शून्याते वेगळे विठ्ठल माझा ॥३॥
Who bestows bliss on bliss Epiphany on epiphany Unadulterated Being in all Vitthal mine	आनंदी आनंद बोधा जेणे बोध । सकळां आत्माशुद्ध विठ्ठल माझा ॥४॥
Origin of the Origin Source of the Absolute Chokha says the Gain Supreme Vitthal mine	मुळाचे निजमूळ अकुळाचे कूळ । चोखा म्हणे निजफळ विठ्ठल माझा ॥५॥

ccc || **4** || ωωω

His visage splendid
Yellow sarong drape
Garland Vaijayanti[1]
Adorning neck

श्रीमुख चांगले
कासे पितांबर ।
वैजयंती हार
रुळे कंठी ॥१॥

He, the Dusky[2], is
My nearest and dearest
Let my eyes see Him
O great Saints

तो माझ्या जीविचा
जिवलग सावळा ।
भेटवा हो डोळां
संतजन ॥२॥

Great many rescued
In so disparate manners
All the Scriptures glorify
His benevolence

बहुतांचे धावणे
केले नानापरी ।
पुराणे ही थोरी
वानिताती ॥३॥

Chokha says Vedas
And Shastras[3] who manifests
He alone protects us
Disparately

चोखा म्हणे वेद
शास्त्रांसी जो साक्षी ।
तोचि आम्हा रक्षी
नानापरी ॥४॥

1 One of the fourteen jewels extracted through the Great Churning of the Sea

2 Vitthal, being an incarnation of Krishna, has the same dark complexion, hence addressed thus.

3 Schools of Indian philosophy also called Darshan

ᲃᲃᲃ || **5** || ᲄᲄᲄ

Unadulterated[1] good, unadulterated good
One and only Pandurang mine

Bliss is at His feet
Reserve of all good deeds

Enormous sins got absolved
Unadulterated goodness of His name

At His door Chokha Mela
Beholds Vitthal with own eyes

•✥•

चोखट चांग चोखट चांग ।
एक माझा पांडुरंग ॥१॥

सुख तयाचे चरणी ।
अवघी सुकृतांची खाणी ॥२॥

महापातकी नासले ।
चोखट नाम हे चांगले ॥३॥

महाद्वारी चोखामेळा ।
विठ्ठल पाहातसे डोळां ॥४॥

•✥•

1 The Marathi word चोखट has familial ties with the Poet's name, Chokha (चोखा), leading to beautiful wordplay throughout the poem. It also bears great significance when one takes into consideration the fact that the community, in which the Poet was born, was considered to be impure by the so-called higher echelons of the society.

ଔଔଔ || **6** || ଈଈଈ

Let's clap with hands Let's raise the flag Let's walk down the path Towards Pandhari	टाळी वाजवावी गुढी उभारावी । वाट हे चालावी पंढरीची ॥१॥
Town square of Pandhari And its public places All are thronged By Varkaris	पंढरीचा हाट कउलांची पेठ । मिळाले चतुष्ट वारकरी ॥२॥
Flocks of flags Converge countless Loud acclamations On the banks of Bhima	पताकांचे भार मिळाले अपार । होतो जयजयकार भीमातीरी ॥३॥
The Name of the Lord Rids of fears and worries So speaks Geeta And Bhagvat	हरिनाम गर्जता भय नाही चिंता । ऐसे बोले गीता भागवत ॥४॥
Come, o fallen, debauched And get purified here Proclaims with faith Chokha Mela	खट नट यावे शुद्ध होऊनि जावे । दवंडी पिटी भावे चोखामेळा ॥५॥

ଓଓଓ || **7** || ଌଌଌ

Chants of Vitthal, Vitthal
Reverberates entire Pandhari

Rings the name of the Lord
Amidst the flocks of flags

Nivrutti, Dnyandev, Sopan[1]
And countless other Vaishnav

Praise of the Lord exuberant
Chokha prostrates on their feet

विठ्ठल विठ्ठल गजरी ।
अवघी दुमदुमली पंढरी ॥१॥

होतो नामाचा गजर ।
दिंड्या पताकांचे भार ॥२॥

निवृत्ति ज्ञानदेव सोपान ।
अपार वैष्णव ते जाण ॥३॥

हरिकीर्तनाची दाटी ।
तेथे चोखा घाली मिठी ॥४॥

1 Dnyandev and his brothers, Nivrutti & Sopan, were Chokha Mela's contemporaries and were accompanied by him on their numerous excursions for the spread of the teachings of the Varkari Sect.

ଓଓଓ || **8** || ଌଌଌ

Wandered a lot	बहुत हिंडलो
From lands to lands	देशदेशांतर ।
But my mind settled	परी मन नाही स्थिर
In none of them	झाले कोठे ॥१॥
Great many holy places	बहुत तीर्थे
Have returned from	फिरोनिया आलो ।
But like my mind	मनासवे झालो
I am raging insane	वेडगळचि ॥२॥
Great many icons	बहुत प्रतिमा
Have seen, heard too	ऐकिल्या पाहिल्या ।
Mind has remained still	मनाच्या राहिल्या
Unrestrained	वेरझारा ॥३॥
Chokha says on seeing	चोखा म्हणे पाहता
Pandhari, the Heaven on earth	पंढरी भूवैकुंठ ।
All agonies of mind	मनाचे हे कष्ट
Have absconded	दूर गेले ॥४॥

ശശശ || 9 || ഌഌഌ

Unadulterated Chokha Mela
Celebrates the name of the Lord

Outcaste Mahar I am
Erstwhile borne as Neel[1]

Slandered the Lord then
Hence reborn as Mahar

Chokha says pollution
Is the fruit of our past deeds

•~•

शुद्ध चोखामेळा ।
करी नामाचा सोहळा ॥१॥

यातीहीन मी महार ।
पूर्वी निळाचा अवतार ॥२॥

कृष्णनिंदा घडली होती ।
म्हणोनि महार जन्मप्राप्ती ॥३॥

चोखा म्हणे विटाळ ।
आम्हा पूर्वीचे हे फळ ॥४॥

•~•

1 One of the great warriors in Lord Rama's Army of the Apes from the Ramayana

|| 10 ||

We experienced bliss
We experienced bliss
We beheld the Lord
Within our body

The Observed vanished
The observer hid
The Lord's miracle
Within our body

The Lord behind and in front
Any place without Him?
In heart, we found the Lord
Within our body

Chokha says the Lord
I beheld in Pandhari
Standing on the brick
By the banks of Bhima

आम्हा आनंद झाला
आम्हा आनंद झाला ।
देवोचि देखिला
देहामाजी ॥१॥

देखणे ऊडाले
पाहणे लपाले ।
देवे नवल केले
देहामाजी ॥२॥

मागे पुढे देव
रिता ठाव कोठे ।
हृदयीच भेटे
देही देव ॥३॥

चोखा म्हणे देव
देखिला पंढरी ।
उभा भीमातीरी
विटेवरी ॥४॥

꧁꧁꧁ || **11** || ꧂꧂꧂

Karma gave up
Religion gave up
All disappeared
Then and there

Mores gave up
Taboos overcame
All disappeared
Then and there

Vedas gave up
Shastras gave up
All disappeared
Then and there

Chokha says mine
Doubt dissolved
Within my body
Found the Lord

●~●

कर्माते वाळिले
धर्माते वाळिले ।
सर्व हारपले
जेथिचे तेथे ॥१॥

विधीते वाळिले
निषेधा गिळिले ।
सर्व हारपले
जेथिचे तेथे ॥२॥

वेदाते वाळिले
शास्त्राते वाळिले ।
सर्व हारपले
जेथिचे तेथे ॥३॥

चोखा म्हणे माझा
संदेह फिटला ।
देहींच भेटला
देव आम्हा ॥४॥

●~●

ଓଓଓ || **12** || ಖಖಖ

Rush forth, O Vithu, do not walk so slow
The priests beat me up, whatever my crime

"How has Vithoba's garland reached your neck?"
They curse me, call me Mahar, "The Lord's been defiled"

The dog at Your door, do not disown me, O Benefactor
Pray, Almighty Lord, you are responsible for me

With folded hands, Chokha entreats the Lord
By these my words, pray, do not get offended

धाव घाली विठु आता चालु नको मंद ।
बडवे मज मारिताती काय झाला अपराध ॥१॥

विठोबाचा हार तुझ्या कंठी कैसा आला ।
शिव्या देती महार म्हणती देव बाटविला ॥२॥

तुमचे दारीचा कुतरा नका मोकलू दातारा ।
अहो चक्रपाणी तुम्ही आहा जीमेदारा ॥३॥

कर जोडोनी चोखा विनवितो देवा ।
बोलिलो उत्तरे परि राग नसावा ॥४॥

ଓଓଓ || **13** || ଌଌଌ

If this is what you intended
Why did you give me birth?

Abandoned me, giving birth
What has so hardened your heart?

Wherever gone in my time of need
To whose rescue have you rushed?

Chokha says, O Lord
Do not disown me, O Keshav

•❧❧•

असेच करणे होते तुला ।
तरी का जन्म दिला मला ॥१॥

जन्म देवोनी सांडीले ।
काहो निष्ठुर मन केले ॥२॥

कोठे गेला माझे वेळी ।
केले कोणाचे सांभाळी ॥३॥

चोखा म्हणे देवा ।
नको मोकलू केशवा ॥४॥

•❧❧•

|| 14 ||

Father you are mine
Mother of the world
Why not show mercy
Any on us?

Why this household
Imposed on me
That separates us
From each other?

Birth, dotage, death
For us joys, sorrows
What pleasure watching
All this, O Lord?

Choked up Chokha
Stands at His door
Entreating the Lord
With folded hands

जनक तू माझा
जननी जगाची ।
करुणा आमुची
का हो नये ॥१॥

कासया संसार
लावियेला पाठी ।
पडलीसे तुटी
तुमची माझी ॥२॥

जन्म जरा मरण
आम्हा सुख दुःख ।
पाहासी कौतुक
काय देवा ॥३॥

गहिंवरुनी चोखा
उभा महाद्वारी ।
विनवी जोडुनी
करी विठोबासी ॥४॥

ଓଓଓ || **15** || ଌଌଌ

Outcaste I am called, O Lord
Not knowing how to serve You

We, the lowly, know only this
To sing Your praise aloud

I wish only for the leftovers
Of the Saints, a humble servant

Chokha says, O Lord
You've accepted wretched me

•∾•

यातिहीन मज म्हणती देवा ।
नकळे करू तुमची सेवा ॥१॥

आम्हा नीचांचे ते काम ।
वाचे गावे सदा नाम ॥२॥

उच्छिष्टाची आस ।
संत दासाचा मी दास ॥३॥

चोखा म्हणे नारायणा ।
पदरी घेतले मज दीना ॥४॥

•∾•

ꕥꕥꕥ || **16** || ꕥꕥꕥ

Lowly caste is mine, O Lord
How would I get to serve You?

They tell me to stay far away
How would I get to meet You?

At the slightest touch of my hand
They observe prompt ablution

O my Govinda, Gopala
Begs for mercy Chokha Mela

हीन याती माझी देवा ।
कैसी घडे तुझी सेवा ॥१॥

मज दूर दूर हो म्हणती ।
तुज भेटू कवण्यारीती ॥२॥

माझा लागताची कर ।
सिंतोडा घेताती करार ॥३॥

माझ्या गोविंदा गोपाळा ।
करुणा भाकी चोखामेळा ॥४॥

|| 17 ||

Without toiling hard
Got exhausted, O Lord
Don't see shelter for me
Anywhere

We are hounded
By our own Karma
Whomever shall we
Hold responsible?

Have got entrapped
In debts of foes
Don't know in quicksand
How got stuck

Chokha says, listen
Lord Resident of Pandhari
Who will rescue us
If not you?

श्रम न करिता
भागलो जी देवा ।
न मिळे विसावा
मज कोठे ॥१॥

लागलेसे कर्म
आमुचे पाठारी ।
आता कोणावरी
बोल ठेऊ ॥२॥

सापडलो वैरि-
याचे भांडवली ।
न कळे चिखली
रोवियेलो ॥३॥

चोखा म्हणे अहो
पंढरीनिवासा ।
तुम्हांविण फांसा
उगवी कोण ॥४॥

|| 18 ||

Whom should we claim
To be ours, O Lord?
Pray, tell us who else
Would rush for us?

You are the Almighty
Of all the Three Worlds
The Lord of the lords
Thence this supplication

You had accepted me
Why forsake me now?
Think through and through
Of this, O my Parents

Dependent of yore
I am yours, O Lord
I beg for Your mercy
Earnestly says Chokha

आम्ही कोणावरी सत्ता
करावी बा पंढरिनाथा ।
होईल साहाता
दुजा तत्वता तो सांगा ॥१॥

तूचि बळिया शिरोमणी
आहेसि त्रिभुवनी ।
देवाधिदेव मुगुटमणि
कींव भाकणे यासाठी ॥२॥

केला माझा अंगिकार
आता का करिता अव्हेर ।
तुमचा तुम्ही साचार
करा विचार मायबापा ॥३॥

जन्मोजन्मींचा पोसणा
तुमचाचि नारायणा ।
भाकितो करुणा
आना मना चोखा म्हणे ॥४॥

ଓଓଓ || 19 || ଌଌଌ

Not seeking respect Nor disrespect Both have relevance None for me	नको मज मान अथवा अपमान । दोहींचे कारण मज नाही ॥१॥
Joys or sorrows Fruits of past deeds Born of Karma Erstwhile	सुख अथवा दुःख संचिताचा ठेवा । संकल्पाचा ठेवा जैसा तैसा ॥२॥
Birth and death Is our destiny In vain to desire, despair After these	जन्म मरण हे तो बांधिले पदरी । वाया हाव भरी येणे संगे ॥३॥
Chokha says this Be my resolution To endure this verity Henceforth	चोखा म्हणे ऐसा नेमियेला नेम । तेचि हे वर्म भोगू आता ॥४॥

ଔଔଔ || **20** || ଖଖଖ

O Lord, why to put me	देवा का हे
In this predicament?	साकडे घातिले ।
Solve this riddle	निवारा हे कोडे
For me, please	माझे तुम्ही ॥१॥
The Mighty should be	समर्थे आपुल्या
True to reputation	नामासी पाहावे ।
You ought to realise this	मनी उमजावे
On Your own	आपुलिया ॥२॥
Outcaste that we are	यातिहीन आम्हा
What rights do we have?	कोण अधिकार ।
Everyone shoos us	अवघे दूरदूर
Far away	करिताती ॥३॥
Chokha says such	चोखा म्हणे ऐसा
Demeaning existence	हीन नरदेह ।
I am in a dilemma	पडिला संदेह
What should I do?	काय करू ॥४॥

ଓଓଓ || **21** || ഇഇഇ

Now for how long
Should I hold back, O Lord?

Have been guarding Your door
You seem to have disowned me

This is no good conduct
Suits Your stature well though

Chokha says what to say
Ruined myself on own accord

आता कोठवरी ।
भीड तुमची धरू हरि ॥१॥

दार राखीत बैसलो ।
तुम्ही दिसे मोकलिलो ॥२॥

ही नीत नव्हे बरी ।
तुमची साजे तुम्हां थोरी ॥३॥

चोखा म्हणे काय बोलो ।
आमुचे आम्ही वाया गेलो ॥४॥

ဖဖဖ || **22** || ဆဆဆ

I am terror stricken
That now nothing will work

Now I am obstructed
By the mightier than the mighty

I seek my own good
I get only pain and anguish

On the path of happiness
I find nothing but sorrows

Whatever my endeavours
Chokha says are shattered

घेतलासे भेव ।
आता न चले उपाव ॥१॥

आता आले आड ।
एकाहुनी एक वाड ॥२॥

पाहे आपुलिया चाडा ।
देखे अवघीच पीडा ॥३॥

सुखाचिया वाटे ।
अवघे दुःखाचेच पेटे ॥४॥

जो जो धरू जाय संग ।
चोखा म्हणे होय भंग ॥५॥

|| **23** ||

Privileged I am
To supplicate at your feet
You the Almighty
You know it well

Among all castes
Created mine the basest
"Pollution, Pollution"
Uttered each moment

No one accepts me
In their company
"Get lost from here"
Says one and all

Chokha says, O Lord
Please accept me
That alone can give
Joy to me

अधिकार माझा
निवेदन पाई ।
तुम्ही तो गोसावी
जाणतसा ॥१॥

अवघ्या वर्णामाजी
हीन केली जाती ।
विटाळ विटाळ म्हणती
क्षणोक्षणी ॥२॥

कोणीही अंगिकार
न करिती माझा ।
दूर हो जा
अवघे म्हणती ॥३॥

चोखा म्हणे मज
तुम्ही घ्या पदरी ।
तरीच मज हरि
सुख होय ॥४॥

ঙঙঙ || **24** || ঌঌঌ

What makes You indulge In discrimination, O Lord? This is what puzzles me To no end	काहो केशिराजा दुजे पै धरिता । हे तो आश्चर्यता वाटे मज ॥१॥
One gets throne One gets robes One has to roam But naked	एकासी आसन एकासी वसन । एक तेचि नग्न फिरताती ॥२॥
One gets coarse food One gets banquets One gets no dried bread Despite pleading	एकासी कदान्न एकासी मिष्टान्न । एका न मिळे कोरान्न मागताची ॥३॥
One gets great wealth One gets kingdom One goes begging Lands to lands	एकासी वैभव राज्याची पदवी । एक गावोगावी भीक मागे ॥४॥
It seems the only justice At Your place is this Chokha says, O Lord Such is my Karma	हाचि न्याय तुमचे दिसतो की घरी । चोखा म्हणे हरी कर्म माझे ॥५॥

|| 25 ||

Wherever I go
I am in bondage
In order to break free
I endeavour ever

But I fail to find
Any solution to it
Evermore I sink
In deeper waters

One after another
Fall strikes on me
Despite trying to evade
What should I do?

Chokha says here
All my efforts fail
Rush forth, my Mother
O Lord Vitthal

जिकडे पाहे तिकडे
बांधलोसे हरी ।
सुटायाचा करी
बहु यत्न ॥१॥

परी ते वर्म
मज न कळे काही ।
अधिकचि डोही
बुडतसे ॥२॥

एका पुढे एक
पडती आघात |
सारिता न सरत
काय करू ॥३॥

चोखा म्हणे येथे
न चलेचि काही ।
धावे माझे आई
विठाबाई ॥४॥

ᗧᗧᗧ || **26** || ᗤᗤᗤ

Why I alone Have to consider this? I do not understand The reason at all	मजचि का करणे लागला विचार । परी वर्म साचार न कळे काही ॥१॥
How to serve You? And express devotion? I fail to understand Detachment any	कैशी करू सेवा आणिक ते भक्ती । न कळे विरक्ती मज काही ॥२॥
Apart from this I have no right How should I Go about it?	आणिक तो दुजा नाही अधिकार । कैसा हा विचार करू आता ॥३॥
Chokha says this I remember all the time Extremely difficult It looks ahead	चोखा म्हणे बहु होती आठवण । कठिण कठिण पुढे दिसे ॥४॥

ଔଔଔ || **27** || ଌଌଌ

Does mother need to be	काय हे मातेसी
Taught by the babe?	बाळे शिकवावे ।
Of her own accord	आपुल्या स्वभावे
Embraces it	वोढतसे ॥१॥
The same it would be	तैसाच प्रकार
At Your place	तुमचीये घरी ।
Thus believing	ऐसीच निर्धारी
Walked all the way	आली वाट ॥२॥
But why it seems today	तेचि आजी दिसे
Gone entirely wrong?	वोखटे का झाले ।
It seems by the power	संचिताचे बळे
Of our past deeds	दिसे ऐसे ॥३॥
Chokha says I do not	चोखा म्हणे हा तो
Blame You at all	तुम्हा नाही बोल ।
Our Karma seems to be	आमुचे सखोल
Overpowering	कर्म दिसे ॥४॥

ଓଓଓ || **28** || ରରର

Patience my mind has
None, none at all, O Lord

Have been so tormented in life
Have turned into springs of sorrows

There may be joy in accepting Fate
But in end it is nothing but sorrow

Became carrier of burdens
By futile pursuits got pillaged

Have mercy, O Lord of Pandhari
Chokha surrenders on Your feet

•◦•

धीर माझे मना ।
नाही नाही नारायणा ॥१॥

बहुचि जाचलो संसारे ।
झालो दुःखाचे पाझरे ॥२॥

भोग भोगणे हे सुख ।
परी शेवटी आहे दुःख ॥३॥

भारवाही झालो ।
वाउग्या छंदा नागवलो ॥४॥

दया करा पंढरीराया ।
चोखा लागतसे पाया ॥५॥

•◦•

ଔଔଔ || **29** || ഌഌഌ

Canine or swine, give me birth as feline
But in the home of Vaishnavas alone

That only can make my heart content
I would not beg then for anything else

Blessed leftovers I will savour ardently
Will keep lying around admiringly

Chokha says anyone going to Pandhari
I will lie prostrate happily at their feet

श्वान अथवा सूकर हो का मार्जार ।
परी वैष्णवांचे घर देई देवा ॥१॥

तेणे समाधान होय माझ्या जीवा ।
न भाकी कींव आणिकासी ॥२॥

उच्छिष्ट प्रसाद सेवीन धणिवरि ।
लोळेन परवरी कवतुकाने ॥३॥

चोखा म्हणे कोणी जाता पंढरीसी ।
दंडवत त्यासी घालीन सुखे ॥४॥

꧁꧁꧁ || 30 || ꧂꧂꧂

How far should I
Keep worrying over?
Why do you, O Lord
Know this not?

Trapped inside the net
Caught by the hook
I suffer infinitely
But in vain

Lust and anger have
Become my masters
Which embarrasses me
Exceedingly

Do not know how
Sorrows as mountains
Joys as mustard seeds
Became for me

Chokha says Your praise
My tongue sings not
Great many desires
Burden my head

•~•

आता कोठवरी
करू विवंचना ।
का हे नारायणा
तुम्हा न कळे ॥१॥

सापडलो जाळीं
गुंतलोसे गळीं ।
जीव हळहळी
वाऊगाचि ॥२॥

कामक्रोधांचे
सापडलो हाती ।
बहुत फजीति
होय तेणे ॥३॥

नेणो कैसे दुःख
पर्वतायेवढे ।
सुख राई पाडे
झाले मज ॥४॥

चोखा म्हणे तुमचे
नाम न ये वाचे ।
बहु संकल्पाचे
वोझे माथा ॥५॥

•~•

ꕥꕥꕥ || **31** || ꕥꕥꕥ

Body is not pure Caste befouled Entirely filthy Vice, virtue	नाही देह शुद्ध याति अमंगळ । अवघे वोंगळ गुण दोष ॥१॥
Whatever I try Is against the mores What anything else Should I speak?	करू जाता विचार अवघा अनाचार । आणिक प्रकार काय बोलू ॥२॥
Tongue is not pure Cannot speak proper Condemned I am By one and all	वाणी नाही शुद्ध धड न ये वचन । धिःकारिती जन सर्व मज ॥३॥
To avoid my touch No one seats near me Chokha says such is Life mine	अंग संग कोणी जवळ न बैसे । चोखा म्हणे ऐसे जीवित माझे ॥४॥

ꕥꕥꕥ || **32** || ꕥꕥꕥ

Whatever good or bad Is destined to me That I will happily Undergo in life	बरे हे वाईट आहे माझे भाळी । ते सुखे हो बळी जीवे माझ्या ॥१॥
Now I am not angry With anyone, O Lord I have accepted My own fate	आता कोणावरी रुसो नये देवा । भोग वो भोगावा आपुलाचि ॥२॥
Consequences of past deeds Make things happen Why to speak in vain Of anything else?	आहे जे संचित तैसे होत जात । वाउगा वृत्तांत बोल काय ॥३॥
Chokha says I am So embarrassed now Whatever wrong happened Was my Karma	चोखा म्हणे आता बहु लाज वाटे । झाले जे वोखटे कर्म माझे ॥४॥

|| 33 ||

When I make efforts
Seeking happiness
All of them futile
Seem to me

Sufferings endless
Mind undergoes
Such unrestrained is
My desire

Everything riddled
Appears to me
Better not to speak this
To anyone

Chokha says I am
In such a dilemma
Deliver me at once
Out of this

सुखाचिया लागी
करितो उपाय ।
तो अवघेचि वाव
दिसो येते ॥१॥

करिता तळमळ
मन हे राहिना ।
अनावर जाणा
वासना हे ॥२॥

अवघेचि साकडे
दिसोनिया आले ।
न बोलावे ते भले
कोणापुढे ॥३॥

चोखा म्हणे मी
पडिलो गुन्हाडी ।
सोडवी तातडी
यांतूनिया ॥४॥

ശശശ || **34** || ഌഌഌ

I will speak such language
That You understand
I am not going to hesitate
At all now

What should I do, O Lord
Smothered by persecution
Even You do not reach out
To my rescue

How long should I
Supplicate, O Lord
All my hopes have
Come crashing

Chokha says now
Enough of false hopes
We alone understand
Our own cause

कळेल तैसे बोल
तुजचि बोलेन ।
भीड मी न धरीन
तुझी काही ॥१॥

काय करू देवा
दाटलो जाचणी ।
न या चक्रपाणी
सोडवण्या ॥२॥

कोठवरी धावा
पोकारू केशवा ।
माझा तव हेवा
खुंटलासे ॥३॥

चोखा म्हणे आता
पुरे चाळवण ।
आमुचे कारण
जाणो आम्ही ॥४॥

ꝏꝏꝏ || **35** || ꝏꝏꝏ

Time and again How much to complain My source of strength Has dried up	वारंवार किती करू करकर । माझा तव आधार खुंटलासे ॥१॥
Not speaking any further That alone would be wise Will become a rock Lying at Your door	न बोलावे आता हेचि शहाणपण । होऊनी पाषाण पडो द्वारी ॥२॥
Someday, sometime You might remember me This only one hope I hold now	केव्हा तरी तुम्हा होईल आठव । हाचि एक भाव करू आता ॥३॥
Chokha says then You will come searching Till then my mind I will harden	चोखा म्हणे मग येशील गिवसित । तो वरी चित्त दृढ करू ॥४॥

௸௸௸ || 36 || ௸௸௸

I am but sold On Your feet Offering to You all Faith and life	मी तो विकलो तुमचिये पायी । जीवभाव सर्वही अर्पियेला ॥१॥
I have done all That could be done You ought to decide About me	माझा मीच झालो उतराई देवा । तुमचे तुम्ही पाहा आम्हांकडे ॥२॥
Nine months mother Carries babe in the womb The very same is this bond Between You and me	नवमास माता वोझे वाहे उदरी । तैसीच ही परी तुमची माझी ॥३॥
If own child begging Goes from lands to lands Who should be ashamed of? Chokha asks	अपत्य आपुले फिरे देशोदेशी । ही लाज कोणासी चोखा म्हणे ॥४॥

ଓଓଓ || **37** || ଽଽଽ

One's own
One ought to look after
Aren't You aware
Of all of this?

आपुल्या आपण
सांभाळोनी घ्यावे ।
आहे नाही ठावे
तुम्हा सर्व ॥१॥

In vain Your boast
Of Your reputation
How many times
Should I say this?

वायाची करणे
लौकिकाचा गोवा ।
कोठवरी देवा
बोलणे हे ॥२॥

Tolerated this
Till sufferings overwhelmed
Only if eaten is digested
It's of use

अंगा नाही आले
तव ते साहाले ।
खादले पचले
तरी ते हित ॥३॥

Chokha says Yours
I have to tell You
Does all this make me
Look small?

चोखा म्हणे तुमचे
तुम्हासी सांगणे ।
माझे यात उणे
काय होते ॥४॥

•ꩰꩰ•

ଔଔଔ || 38 || ଋଋଋ

I don't understand why
Your heart has hardened
I don't know which
Of my past deeds

How much should I
Recollect my past
That it is affecting
My future

Now it is difficult
Seems unattainable
My mind's mind too
Is engulfed in worries

Chokha says I don't know
What to do
How to assuage
My desire

●꩜●

नेणो तुमचे मन
कठिण का झाले ।
मज काही न कळे
पूर्व कर्म ॥१॥

किती आठवण
मागिलाची करू ।
तेणे पडे विचारू
पुढीलासी ॥२॥

आता अवघड
दिसते कठीण ।
मनाचे हे मन
चिंता डोही ॥३॥

चोखा म्हणे काय
करू ते आठवेना ।
निवांत वासना
कई होय ॥४॥

●꩜●

ઌઌઌ || 39 || ઌઌઌ

I get no assurance	काही तरी अभय
Nor any reply	न मिळे उत्तर ।
Why have you become	ऐसे का निष्ठुर
So callous	झाला तुम्ही ॥१॥
I call You out	मी तो कळवळोनी
With all my passion	मारितसे हाक ।
What does make You	तुम्हा पडे धाक
So frightened?	कासयाचा ॥२॥
Say few words to me	बोलोनि उत्तरे
That will satisfy me	करी समाधान ।
That is all benefaction	एवढेचि दान
I ask from You	मज द्यावे ॥३॥
Chokha says fulfil	चोखा म्हणे माझी
This wish of mine	पुरवावी आस ।
Make me not despair	न करी उदास
O my Mother	माझे माये ॥४॥

ॐॐॐ || **40** || ॐॐॐ

Now whimpering	आता कणकण
No more in vain	न करी वाउगी ।
What was to happen	होणार ते जगी
Has happened already	होउनी गेले ॥१॥
Wherever I be	दारी परवरी
Dependent I am	झालोसे पोसणा ।
And You mercy	तुम्हांसी करुणा
Show none	न ये काही ॥२॥
Fate takes its course	होयाचे ते झाले
Why to despair	असो का उदास ।
We will live happily	धरोनिया आस
With our hopes	राहो सुखी ॥३॥
Chokha says, to me	चोखा म्हणे मज
This seems to be better	हेचि बरे दिसे ।
No trouble at all	न लावी पिसे
To my mind	जिवा काही ॥४॥

ଔଔଔ || 41 || ൽൽൽ

I need not salvation Or the stay in Heaven Happily in Pandhari I will live	न लगे भुक्ति मुक्ति वैकुंठीचा वास । सुखे पंढरीस राहीन देवा ॥१॥
Whatever hardships I may have to bear But leaving Pandhari I will go nowhere	आणिक साकडे घडोत नानापरी । परी सोडोनी पंढरी न वजे कोठे ॥२॥
Even if I don't get Food to eat here I will readily survive On water	खावयासी जरी न मिळेचि अन्न । उदक सेवीन धणिवरी ॥३॥
Let people abhor Let them call me fool That would not hamper My worship	कोणी निंदो कोणी म्हणोत का वेडा । जेणे नव्हे पीडा भजनासी ॥४॥
Chokha says this is All the bliss I seek Sorrows and miseries Anyplace else	चोखा म्हणे मज आहे हेच सुख । आणिके ठायी दुःख नानापरी ॥५॥

ଓଓଓ || **42** || ରରର

How do I praise How do I praise How do I meditate Pandurang?	कैसा मी वानू कैसा मी वानू । कैसा ध्याना आणू पांडुरंग ॥१॥
Which way do I Worship my Lord? Never is my mind At peace at all	कैसी ते सेवा करू ते प्रकार । नव्हेचि अंतर स्थिर माझे ॥२॥
Restraining this mind Does not come to hand How much do I Worry over it?	वारिता हे मन न येचि हाता । कितीसी हे चिंता करू आता ॥३॥
Chokha says here All efforts are futile How would I find His feet?	चोखा म्हणे येथे खुंटला उपाय । कैसेनि पाय आतुडती ॥४॥

ଓଓଓ || 43 || ଌଌଌ

All alone, seated with me Speaks of joys and sorrows Holding my chin Pacifies me	एकांती बैसोनि करी गुज गोष्टी । धरोनि हनुवटी बुझावित ॥१॥
Pray, do not be Offended by life I will tell you The essence	नको बा मानू संसाराचा शीण । तुज एक खूण सांगतो मी ॥२॥
Whatever that happens Or that does not And joys and sorrows Consequence of Karma	होणार ते होय न होणार ते न होय । सुख दुःख पाहे कर्माधिन ॥३॥
The Lord says, o Chokha Do not be offended Swear this to me, my dearest On my name	देव म्हणे चोख्या नको मानू शीण । तुज माझी आण भक्तराया ॥४॥

|| **44** ||

Why do you consider
Sorrows to be mountains?
I will fulfil wishes
All of yours

The bliss at My door
That is a trove of bliss
Which Namdev already
Has received

That same bliss I will
Bestow upon you
I will bless you
With my grace

You are My life
Dearest of My heart
I will not ever at all
Desert you

Chokha says, O Lord
Indulge my yearning
Hold me close
O Gracious Lord

कासया मानिसी
दुःखाचे पर्वत ।
पुरवीन हेत
सर्व तुझा ॥१॥

महाद्वारी सुख
सुखाची जे राशी ।
ते नामयासी
प्राप्त झाले ॥२॥

त्या सुखाचा अधिकारी
तुज मी करीन ।
दृष्टी हे ठेवीन
तुजवरी ॥३॥

तू माझा प्राण
जिवाचा आवडता ।
तुज मी तत्वता
न विसंबे ॥४॥

चोखा म्हणे देवा
पुरवी माझा लळा ।
न विसंबे दयाळा
मजलागी ॥५॥

ଓଓଓ || **45** || ୡୡୡ

Why should I raise	कासया करू
Mountains of meditation	तपाचे डोंगर ।
Or any of the other	आणिक अपार
Endless rituals?	व्रतदान ॥१॥
Why should I go	कासया जाऊ
Far into the wilderness?	दूर दिगंतरी ।
Rather in Pandhari	राहीन पंढरी
Be a beast	पशुयाती ॥२॥
Why should I observe	कासया उपवास
Fasting and breaking it?	निराहार पारणे ।
Rather seek company of saints	संतसंग पेणे
All the life	जन्मोजन्मीं ॥३॥
Why should I bother	कासया विधि
About mores and taboos?	निषेधाची मात ।
Blissful is companionship	सुखाचा सांगात
Yours and mine	तुमचा माझा ॥४॥
Why should I roam	कासया भ्रमण
Holy places far off?	देशतीर्थाटणी ।
Rather savour stay	सेवीन पायवणी
With saints	संतांघरी ॥५॥
Why should I indulge	कासया करावे
In fire-offering rituals	पंचाग्नि साधन ।
Rather eat leftovers	उच्छिष्ट भक्षीन
At the door of saints	संताद्वारी ॥६॥
Chokha says bliss	चोखा म्हणे सुख
Thus will come home	येईल घरासी ।
Surrendering at the feet	जाईन संतांसी
Of saints, O Lord	शरण देवा ॥७॥

॥ 46 ॥

Companion You are mine for eternity
Why have you put me in such doubts
I do not find joy or solace anywhere
Except only in Pandhari

Vithoba, do You not know this?
You are the Soul of the world
The Origin and the Supreme Being
Still You ignore the wretched

Pray, there is no justice at Your place
One undergoes sorrows, one rules kingdoms
This is not good conduct at all
It does not become Your reputation

Chokha says how puzzling this is
We understand none of Your deeds
Neither Your grace nor Your wrath
We comprehend, O Vithoba

जन्मोजन्मींचे तुम्ही सांगाती ।
काहो मज घातिले भ्रांती ।
नाही कोठे सुख विश्रांति ।
पंढरीवाचोनी सर्वथा ॥१॥

विठोबा का न कळे तुम्हा ।
सर्व जगाचा तू आत्मा ।
पुराण पुरुष परमात्मा ।
आम्हां दीना उपेक्षिसी ॥२॥

पाहा न्याय नाही तुमचे घरी ।
एका दुःख एक राज्य करी ।
ऐसी नीत नव्हे बरी ।
साजे थोरी थोरपणे ॥३॥

चोखा म्हणे नवलाव ।
आम्हा न कळे ठाव भाव ।
तुमचा कैसा घाव डाव ।
काहीच तो विठोबा ॥४॥

ꕥꕥꕥ || **47** || ꕥꕥꕥ

My mind has Resolved this Nothing else I would know	माझ्या तो मने केलासे विचार । आणिक प्रकार नेणे काही ॥१॥
Singing the praise Of the Lord oft No need to fear Anyone then	नाम वेळोवेळा आठवावे वाचे । दुजे आणिकाचे भय नाही ॥२॥
I adore deeply The Lord's feet Now none else Comes to mind	आवडी बैसली विठूचे चरणी । आता दुजेपणी नाही गोष्टी ॥३॥
Chokha says the saints Have made me firm Hence my mind Is at peace	चोखा म्हणे दृढ केलासे संती । म्हणोनी विश्रांती जीवा झाली ॥४॥

ශශශ || **48** || ඞඞඞ

Seeing a Varkari
On way to Pandhari
I will place my forehead
On their feet

With joy, I will
Meet them fondly
Goodness of their hearts
I will rejoice

My parents those
My kith and kin too
I will devote to them
My very existence

Chokha says they are
Source of the Gain Supreme
My saviours of yore
For eternity

कोणी पंढरीसी
जाती वारकरी ।
तयांचे पायांवरी
भाळ माझे ॥१॥

आनंदे तयांसी
भेटेन आवडी ।
अंतरीची गोडी
घेईन सुख ॥२॥

ते माझे मायबाप
सोयरे सज्जन ।
तयां तनु मन
वोवाळीन ॥३॥

चोखा म्हणे ते
माहेर निजाचे ।
जन्मोजन्मांतरिचे
साहाकारी ॥४॥

ଓଓଓ || **49** || ଛଛଛ

My anguish, fatigue Vanished entirely Seeing Vithoba On the brick	माझा शिण भाग अवघा हरपला । विठोबा देखिला विटेवरी ॥१॥
My life has become Meaningful now Having seen His feet To heart's content	अवघ्या जन्मांचे सार्थक पै झालें । समचरण देखिले डोळेभरी ॥२॥
On Chandrabhaga[1] banks Varkaris dance Singing the Lord's praise With a great joy	चंद्रभागे तीरी नाचती वारकरी । विठ्ठलनामगजरी आनंदाने ॥३॥
Flags and emblems Flock endlessly Amidst the acclamations Of the Lord's name	दिंड्या गरुड टके पताकांचे भार । होतो जयजयकार नामघोष ॥४॥
Such joyous celebrations Rare even for gods We get effortlessly Chokha says	तो सुखसोहळा देवांसी दुर्लभ । आम्हा तो सुलभ चोखा म्हणे ॥५॥

1 At Pandharpur, River Bhima takes the shape of a crescent moon, hence the name चंद्रभागा, i.e. the Crescent-shaped.

ଓଓଓ || **50** || ଌଌଌ

O my mind, make This one resolution Do not indulge in Anything else	माझ्या मना तू धरी का विचार । न करी प्रकार आन काही ॥१॥
Those Varkaris Who go to Pandhari Happily become a beast At their home	पंढरीसी कोणी जाती वारकरी । सुखे त्यांचे घरी पशुयाती ॥२॥
In their company Contemplation happens Bathing in Chandrabhaga On Ekadashi[1]	तयाचिया सवे घडेल चिंतन । चंद्रभागे स्नान एकादशी ॥३॥
Singing the Lord's praise In the company of saints Will be an effortless Gain for me	जागर क्षिरापती वैष्णव सांगाते । घडेल आपैते लाभ मज ॥४॥
Chokha says owing to The company of saints I will get to join feasts Along with the rest[2]	चोखा म्हणे घडेल संतांची संगती । सहज पंगती बैसेन मी ॥५॥

1 The eleventh day of Indian lunar calendar which is considered as the sacred most by the Varkaris.

2 The poet here is referring to the fact that despite his Sainthood, he was never allowed to mingle with others by the so-called upper castes. It was only in the company of the Varkari Saints, that the Poet got equal treatment.

ଔଔଔ || 51 || ଌଌଌ

They are my kindred
Benefactors, companions
Whoever constantly
Remember Vithoba

In their company
Benefits great many
I found the treasure
In the form of Pandurang

Of the past and future
Got relieved of worries
My near and dear ones
Having met

In their company
Solace and bliss
Whosoever constantly
Remember Vithoba

Chokha says they relieve
From worldly anxieties
The Lord of Vaikuntha[1]
They make visible

●~●

ते माझे सोयरे
सज्जन सांगाती ।
जे आठविती
विठोबासी ॥१॥

तयांचे संगती
बहु लाभ झाला ।
ठेवा जो जोडला
पांडुरंग ॥२॥

मागिला पुढिला
झाला परिहार ।
ते माझे माहेर
भेटलेसे ॥३॥

तयांचे संगती
सुखाची विश्रांती ।
जे का आठविती
विठोबासी ॥४॥

चोखा म्हणे ते
भवाचे तारक ।
वैकुंठनायक
दाखविती ॥५॥

●~●

1 Lord Vishnu's celestial abode wherein His devotees are believed to attain Salvation.

ଔଔଔ || **52** || ଋଋଋ

Shame on that conduct	धिक् तो आचार
Shame on that thought	धिक् तो विचार ।
Shame on that life	धिक् तो संसार
Shame on having borne	धिक् जन्म ॥१॥
Shame on that learning	धिक् ते पठण
Shame on those scriptures	धिक् ते पुराण ।
Shame on all rituals	धिक् यज्ञ हवन
Those carried out	केले तेणे ॥२॥
Shame on that knowledge	धिक् ब्रह्मज्ञान
Futile is this talk	वाउग्या ह्या गोष्टी ।
Without imbibing kindness	दया क्षमा पोटी
Forgiveness and peace	शांति नाहीं ॥३॥
Shame on that meditation	धिक् ते आसन
Shame on those grown hair	जटाभार माथा ।
Futile is all this routine	वायाचि हे कंथा
Thus followed	धरिली जेणे ॥३॥
Chokha says shame	चोखा म्हणे धिक्
On such a man ever borne	जन्मला तो नर ।
Hell infinite for him	भोगी नरक घोर
In the end	अंतकाळी ॥४॥

॥ 53 ॥

In the company of sandalwood	चंदनाच्या संगे
Even thorny trees	बोरीया बाभळी ।
And wild shrubs smell sweet	हेकळी टाकळी
Like sandalwood	चंदनची ॥१॥
In the company of saints	संतांचिया संगे
The faithless people	अभाविक जन ।
Are turned into saints	तयांच्या दर्शने
Themselves too	तेचि होती ॥२॥
Chokha says know this	चोखा म्हणे ऐसा
The essence of spirituality	परमार्थ साधावा ।
Otherwise be the beast	नाही तरी भार वाहावा
Of burden	खरा ऐसा ॥३॥

ଓଓଓ || **54** || ହହହ

Mind is immersed	अखंड समाधी
In endless Samadhi[1]	होउनी ठेले मन ।
Remembrance of body	गेले देहभान
Having forgotten	विसरोनी ॥१॥
Fear of taboos, mores	विधिनिषेध भेणे
Does not affect Samadhi	न मोडे समाधी ।
Disappeared vainglory	तुटली उपाधी
Of possessions	लिगाडाची ॥२॥
Carrying out chores	चालता बोलता
Does not affect Samadhi	न मोडे समाधी ।
Absolute purity of mind	मूळ अंतरशुद्धी
Is the only reason	कारण हे ॥३॥
Chokha says such is	चोखा म्हणे ऐसा
The occasion of Samadhi	समाधी सोहळा ।
Knows the peerless	जाणे तो विरळा
One in a million	लक्षामाजी ॥४॥

1 The state of being in perfect unison with the Supreme Being and the Creation.

ଔଔଔ || 55 || ଋଋଋ

Beauty of the eye the vision perceived
The eye popped out for the sake of beauty

Beauty of the eye perceived the eye
Inevitably there got closed the eye

Chokha says how wondrous it is
Having perceived beauty the eye dissolved

•~•

डोळियाचा देखणा पाहता दिठी ।
डोळाच निघाला देखण्या पोटी ॥१॥

डोळियाचा देखणा पाहिला डोळा ।
आपेआप तेथ झाकला डोळा ॥२॥

चोखा म्हणे नवलाव झाला ।
देखणा पाहता डोळा विराला ॥३॥

•~•

ශශශ || **56** || ඍඍඍ

Beyond body, mind; it came to be
The Formless in a form stood here

Behold the Lord, pray all, behold the Lord
Behold the Lord, pray all, within own body

Uncovered Lord manifested in the world
What was naked that engulfed the Lord

Chokha says naked and uncovered became One
Behold, how effortlessly selfhood dissolved

देह बुद्धीवेगळे जे आकारले ।
निर्गुण ते सगुणपणे उभे ठेले ॥१॥

देव पहा तुम्ही देव पहा तुम्ही ।
देव पहा तुम्ही आपुले देही ॥२॥

उघडाचि देवो जगी प्रकाशला ।
नागव्या भक्ताने देव ग्रासिला ॥३॥

चोखा म्हणे नागवे उघडे एक झाले ।
सहज मीपण देख मावळले ॥४॥

ଓଓଓ || **57** || ଓଓଓ

Within own body, beheld Pandhari
Soul immortal standing on the brick

Know Him to be the Lord manifest
Peace is Rukmini, the divine consort

Whatever has form gets destroyed
Soul immortal remains Vitthal

Thus the Lord held in his heart
Chokha Mela is welded to His feet

देही देखिली पंढरी ।
आत्मा अविनाश विटेवरी ॥१॥

तो हा पांडुरंग जाणा ।
शांति रुक्मिणि निजांगना ॥२॥

आकारले तितुके नासे ।
आत्मा अविनाश विठ्ठल दिसे ॥३॥

ऐसा विठ्ठल हृदयी ध्यायी ।
चोखा मेळा जडला पायी ॥४॥

|| 58 ||

Let Mind be
On the Lord
Who resolution
Makes this?

Sense of body
When forgotten
The Lord too
Got dissolved

Inferior is Being
Worship superior
Thence is born
Discrimination

To begin with, exists
No Chokha Mela
How can exist
Pollution?

पांडुरंगी
लागो मन ।
कोण चिंतन
करी ऐसे ॥१॥

देहभाव
विसरला ।
देव गेला
बुडोनी ॥२॥

जीव उपाधि
भक्ती वंद्य ।
तेथे भेद
जन्मला ॥३॥

मुळीच चोखा
मेळा नाही ।
कैंचा राही
विटाळ ॥४॥

ॐॐॐ || 59 || ॐॐॐ

In the ocean of faith	भावसमुद्री
Loaded cargo vessel	भरियेले केणे ।
Arrived currency	आणियेले नाणे
Of Dvaraka[1]	द्वारकेचे ॥१॥
On all the twelve routes	बाराही मार्गांची
Carries out trade	वणीज्ज करी ।
In the city of Pandhari	पंढर हे पुरी
Namdev[2]	नामदेव ॥२॥
Chokha says let us	चोखा म्हणे
Prostrate at his feet	लोटांगणी जाऊ ।
Let us behold Namdev	नामदेव पाहू
Dearest to the Lord	केशवाचा ॥३॥

1 The ancient capital city of the Yadav Empire of which Lord Krishna was one of the princes. According to the Varkari legends, Lord Krishna preferred Pandharpur over Dvaraka and settled therein, immersing the latter in the sea.

2 Sant Namdev spread the teachings of the Varkari Sect all over the Indian subcontinent by traversing its length & breadth, performing kirtan at each stop during his journeys. The Poet is referring to this contribution of his Guru in this poem.

ꕥꕥꕥ || **60** || ꕥꕥꕥ

You have resolved So many predicaments Why should I speak Contrarily?	तुम्ही तो सांकडे बहुत वारिले । आता का उगले बोलू देवा ॥१॥
Till date I was entrapped By the mess of sensations That is what seems to have Caused embarrassment	आजीवरी पडिलो लिगाडाचे गुंती । तेणेचि फजिती झाली दिसे ॥२॥
I see the path Opened wide for me Despite the condemnation Of the world	झाला दिसे मज मोकळा मारग । धिक्कारिती जग मागे पुढे ॥३॥
Chokha says witnessed This strange happening That has truly impinged On my mind	चोखा म्हणे ऐसे विपरीत देखिले । ते साचचि संचले मनी माझ्या ॥४॥

ೞೞೞ || 61 || ೞೞೞ

Anyone who comes Under its spell It wreaks havoc On them	याचिया छंदा जे लागले प्राणी । त्यांची धुळधाणी केली येणे ॥१॥
Enough of its sway Enough of its sway All it leaves behind Are endless desires	याचा संग पुरे याचा संग पुरे । अंतरी ते उरे हांव हांव ॥२॥
It deviates the self From the path of spirituality How much to persuade This urchin	स्वार्थ परमार्था घातिलासे चिरा । किती फजीतखोरा बुझवावे ॥३॥
Forbidden places It stubbornly visits It does what is untoward Unrestrained	न जावे तेथे हाटेची जाय । करू नये ते करी सय न धरी काही ॥४॥
Chokha says, o mind Swear by yourself Find contentment For an instant	चोखा म्हणे तुज तुझीच आण । होई समाधान घटिका भरी ॥५॥

ଓଓଓ || **62** || ଌଌଌ

Just like an ape	माकडाचे परी
Keeps shaking head	हालविती मान ।
Boasts of glory	दावी थोरपण
In the world	जगामध्ये ॥१॥
Unaware of own good	स्वहिता मुकले
Unaware of own good	स्वहिता मुकले ।
Closes eyes with force	बळे झाकी डोळे
Holds nose[1]	नाक धरी ॥२॥
Beads and postures	माळा आणि मुद्रा
Such masquerades	दाविताती सोंग ।
Swinging bodies	डोलविती अंग
But no essence	रंग नाही ॥३॥
Hounded by hunger	पोटाचा पोसणा
Creates façade	विटंबना करी ।
Goes asking for alms	भीक दारोदारी
Door to door	मागतसे ॥४॥
Chokha says such	चोखा म्हणे ऐसे
Fraudsters in the world	जगामध्ये भोंदु ।
Who would call them	तया कोण साधु
Sadhu, O Lord?	म्हणे देवा ॥५॥

1 Here, the reference is to the fake yogis who know nothing beyond physical maneuvers like *asanas* and *mudras*.

ღღღ || **63** || ꩜꩜꩜

Elaborate banquet Sitting to feast on Houseflies kill The appetite	षड्रस पक्कान्न भोजनी बैसता । मक्षिके तत्त्वता घात केला ॥१॥
Ultimate nature When debased What to expect Otherwise	जातीचा स्वभाव अमंगळ आहे । कवणे तेथे लाहे भिन्न भिन्न ॥२॥
Nature of the dog Even when seated on throne Goes looking for But excreta	श्वानाचा स्वभाव बैसताहि गादी । नरकादि शुद्धि पाहो धावे ॥३॥
Does not recognize Own and strangers Barks incessantly By nature	आपुले पारखे न कळेचि तया । भुके भलतिया स्वभावेचि ॥४॥
Chokha says such Is the life of the wicked Ever despicable In the world	चोखा म्हणे तैसे दुर्जनाचे जिणे । सदा लाजिरवाणे जनांमध्ये ॥५॥

ଔଔଔ || **64** || ଔଔଔ

In the company of the low-born The Lord became polluted By cleansing with water Made Him pure	नीचाचे संगती देवो विटाळला । पाणीये प्रक्षाळोनि सोवळा केला ॥१॥
To begin with, pure Is the Lord at all? It's like making the eye To see the eye	मुळीच सोवळा कोठे तो वोवळा । पाहता पाहाणे डोळा जयापरी ॥२॥
Within the pure Resides the Pure Why doesn't the impure Reside in the impure?	सोवळ्याचे ठाई सोवळा आहे । वोवळ्या ठाई वोवळा का न राहे ॥३॥
Chokha says the Lord Is above the both To the content of my eyes Him I beheld	चोखा म्हणे देव दोहींच्या वेगळा । तोचि म्या देखिला दृष्टीभरी ॥४॥

ꢃꢃꢃ || **65** || ꢂꢂꢂ

Equally polluting are
All Five Elements[1]
That the entire world
Is made of

पंचही भूतांचा
एकचि विटाळ ।
अवघाचि मेळ
जगी नांदे ॥१॥

Then how can one be pure
And the other impure
If the origin of pollution
Is our bodies?

तेथे तो सोवळा
वोवळा तो कोण ।
विटाळाचे कारण
देह मूळ ॥२॥

In the beginning and end
Nothing but pollution
Pure can be anyone
Which way?

आदिअंती अवघा
विटाळ संचला ।
सोवळा तो झाला
कोण न कळे ॥३॥

Chokha says to me
This puzzles a lot
Beyond pollution
Is anyone at all?

चोखा म्हणे मज
नवल वाटते ।
विटाळा परते
आहे कोण ॥४॥

1 The five elements of nature: Earth, Air, Fire, Water & Sky. All the human beings, just like the remainder of the Creation, are said to be formed out of these Five Great Elements.

ଔଔଔ || **66** || ଌଌଌ

Who be the pure? Who be the impure? Beyond the both Vitthal mine	कोण तो सोवळा कोण तो वोवळा । दोहींच्या वेगळा विठ्ठल माझा ॥१॥
Who got polluted? By which means? Conceived essentially As the Pure	कोणासी विटाळ कशाचा जाहला । मुळीचा संचला सोवळाची ॥२॥
Pollution of the Five[1] Within one body Then pure in the world How can be any?	पाचांचा विटाळ येकाचिये आंगा । सोवळा तो जगा- माजी कोण ॥३॥
Chokha says mine Vitthal alone is pure Despite being formless Stands on the brick	चोखा म्हणे माझा विठ्ठल सोवळा । अरूपे आगळा विटेवरी ॥४॥

1 The Five Great Elements.

∞∞∞ || 67 || ∞∞∞

Polluted by Time
Both the being and the Beyond
Confined to this world
With unyielding bonds

Pollution, pollution
All over the universe
Encompasses living, non-living
Nothing but pollution

Pollution in joys
Pollution in sorrows
Pollution in pollution
Has thrived

The womb of pollution
Bears the fruit of pollution
Chokha the unadulterated
Sings the Lord's praise

•∞•

काळाचा विटाळ
जीवशिवा अंगी ।
बांधलासे जगी
दृढ गाठी ॥१॥

विटाळी विटाळ
चवदाही भुवनी ।
स्थावर जंगम व्यापुनी
विटाळची ॥२॥

सुखासी विटाळ
दुःखासी विटाळ ।
विटाळीं विटाळ
वाढलासे ॥३॥

विटाळाचे अंगी
विटाळाचे फळ ।
चोखा तो निर्मल
नाम गाय ॥४॥

•∞•

|| 68 ||

Once such a wonder happened
The Lord unexpectedly arrived

Arriving, sat on the verandah
Said, "Give me something to eat"

Jani[1] said, "O dear Lord
Go, have by Your own hands"

The Lord searched everything
Found the earthen pot covered

Rushing forth the Lord went
Returned with broken rice

Holding Jani's hand
Put morsels in her mouth

Both happily had the meal
Belching with contentment

Chokha stood outside
Begging for the leftovers

एकदा ऐसे नवल झाले ।
देव अकल्पित आले ॥१॥

येवोनी बैसले परवरी ।
म्हणे देई काही नेहरी ॥२॥

जनी म्हणे देवराया ।
आपुल्या हाते घेई सखया ॥३॥

देवे अवघे पाहिले ।
तो झाकणी झाकण ठेविले ॥४॥

लाहे लाहे देव गेला ।
झाकणी कण्या घेऊनी आला॥५॥

धरोनी जनीचा हात ।
घास घालीत मुखांत ॥६॥

दोघे जेवोनिया धाले ।
तृप्तीचे ते ढेकर दिले ॥७॥

चोखा उभा तो बाहेरी ।
उष्ट्यासाठी पदर पसरी ॥८॥

1 Sant Namdev's maidservant, Jani or Janabai was a Saint-poet of highest caliber, perhaps the first woman to speak against patriarchy in her poems.

ଓଓଓ || **69** || ଓଓଓ

Here I have company Only of the wicked That saddens me All the time	येथे तो संग आहे दुर्जनांचा । म्हणोनी शीण त्याचा होत आहे ॥१॥
My own community Have to eat impious Liquor and meat Their meals comprise	यातीचा प्रकार अमंगळ खाणार । मद्य मांस आहार करिताती ॥२॥
Others call me names Speaking out filth That hurts my heart To no end	मुखे ते वाईट बोलती कश्मळ । तेणे हळहळ जीव करी ॥३॥
Chokha says thus I am to go nowhere Pray, how long should I Suffer all this?	चोखा म्हणे ऐसा पडिलो काचणी । सोसू हे जाचणी कोठवरी ॥४॥

ꕥꕥꕥ || **70** || ꕥꕥꕥ

Such are the ways Of this world What should I say Of its vices, virtues?	बहुत प्रकार बहुत या जगाचे । काय वानू त्याचे गुणदोष ॥१॥
Debased is the caste Nameless existence How can one be kith Or kin to anyone?	नीच हे याति अनामिक नाव । तेथे भावाभाव कोण कैचा ॥२॥
Sycophants, thieves, womanizers Corrupt through and through Debased existence for eternity Is their destiny	चाहाड चोर जार भ्रष्ट ते साचे । हीनत्व जन्मांचे पदरीं आहे ॥३॥
Chokha says I suffer In the company of such Separation from you Anguishes me	चोखा म्हणे त्यांचे संगती पडिलो । बहू हे पीडिलो वियोगाने ॥४॥

ଔଔଔ || **71** || ଈଈଈ

Here for me nothing	येथे तो दुःखाचे
But mountains of sorrows	डोंगर आठवती ।
My mind bewails	वाटतसे खंती
All the while	मना माझ्या ॥१॥
O Lord Resident of Pandhari	काहो पंढरीराया
Why have you sent me away?	परदेशी केले ।
I find none of my own here	कोणी न देखे आपुले
What do I do?	काय करू ॥२॥
I long for Pandhari	आठवे पंढरी
I long for Your door	आठवे महाद्वार ।
Gatherings of the saints	संताचा भार
I long for	आठवतो ॥३॥
I long for Namdev	आठवतो नामा
Pundalik dearest	पुंडलिक सखा ।
Chokha says behold	चोखा म्हणे देखा
I lie in distress	तळमळ वाटे ॥४॥

ଔଔଔ || **72** || ଌଌଌ

Whenever I will be released	केधवा सुटेन
This my mind thinks ever	ऐसे जाले जीवा ।
Why am I entrapped	गोवियेले देवा
Here, O Lord?	काहो येथे ॥१॥
Now please rush	आता झडकरी
To my rescue	धावे लवकरी ।
Release me, O Hari	सोडवी बा हरी
From here	मजलागी ॥२॥
Upon my life	प्राण हा कंठी
I beseech You	धरीला तुजसाठी ।
What makes You	निर्वाण दृष्टी
Take so long?	पाहसी काय ॥३॥
Chokha says waste	चोखा म्हणे वाया
No time further	चालिलासे वेळ ।
I see my end	आला असे काळ
Pretty nigh	निकट दिसे ॥४॥

|| 73 ||

My end is nigh
It seems to me
What was destined
Has happened

From birth, dependent
Have been servant Yours
Now in the end
I lie far away

Have lost all hopes
Of Your leftovers
Fate has taken
Its course

Chokha says mine
Prostration at Your feet
Take me in shelter
Of Your grace

माझा तो समय
निकट दिसे आला ।
लेख तो लेखिला
तैसे झाले ॥१॥

जन्मोनी पोसणा
तुमचाच दास ।
आता निकट सहवास
अंतरलो ॥२॥

उच्छिष्टाची आस
सरलीसे दिसे ।
प्रारब्धासरसे
वोढवले ॥३॥

चोखा म्हणे माझा
दंडवत पायीं ।
करी आता साई
कृपेची तू ॥४॥

ഌഌഌ || **74** || ഌഌഌ

Unrestrained mind
Brings on frenzy
Goes wandering far
Beyond reach

Upon its feet
Put shackles firm
No more troubles
From it then

It will stay ever still
Such is this measure
Know not ways
Any other

Chokha says whatever
You have taught
That has borne fruit
O Namdev

•~•

मोकाट हे मन
करीत बावरे ।
हिंडता वावरे
न सापडेचि ॥१॥

तयाचिये पायी
दृढ घाली बेडी ।
न करी वोढावोढी
कोणी मग ॥२॥

निवांतचि राहे
ऐसा हा उपाय ।
नेणे आन सोय
दुजी काही ॥३॥

चोखा म्हणे तुम्ही
जे जे शिकविले ।
तेचि फळा आले
नामदेवा ॥४॥

•~•

ೞೞೞ || 75 || ೲೲೲ

Absolute love	अवघ्याचि लोभे
Brought the Absolute	अवघेचि आले ।
The Absolute assumed	अवघे संचले
The form Absolute	अवघे रूप ॥१॥
Absolute endearing	अवघे गोजिरे
Absolute elegant	अवघे साजिरे ।
Absolute dissolves	अवघ्या परिहारे
In the Absolute	अवघेचि ॥२॥
Absolute bliss	अवघे आनंदाचे
From the Absolute	अवघेचि वोतिले ।
Absolute manifestation	अवघे प्रकाशले
Of the Absolute	अवघेपणे ॥३॥
Chokha says the Absolute	चोखा म्हणे अवघे
Revealed to Namdev	नामया फावले ।
The Absolute he showed	अवघेचि दाविले
To me as well	तेणे मज ॥४॥

❧❧❧ || 76 || ❧❧❧

What to perceive
What to worship
What to sing
For whom

Where to go
Where to stay
Where to look
For what

Where be joy
Where be sorrow
Where to seek
All of which

Chokha says
Namdev judicious
Sensed the conundrum
Conveyed to me

काय पाहू
काय ध्याऊ ।
काय गाऊ
कवनाते ॥१॥

कोठे जाऊ
कोठे राहू ।
कोठे पाहू
काय ते ॥२॥

कोठे सुख
कोठे दुःख ।
कोठे अवघे
पाहणे देख ॥३॥

चोखा म्हणे
नामया सुजाण ।
वोळखोनी खुण
सांगे मज ॥४॥

ଓଓଓ || **77** || ଌଌଌ

Golden is this day
Of great fortune
I met in person
Namdev

आजि सोनियाचा
दिवस धन्य झाला ।
प्रत्यक्ष भेटला
नामदेव ॥१॥

Mine he gave me
Mine he gave me
Mine he gave me
Bliss of love

माझे मज दिले
माझे मज दिले ।
माझे मज दिले
प्रेमसुख ॥२॥

Much longing
After great efforts
My mind brims with
Bliss of bliss

बहुत आटणी
करिता दाटणी ।
सुखाचे सुख मनी
कोंदाटले ॥३॥

The Lord mine he showed
Within my own being
Dissolved then and there
Sense of selfhood

माझा मज देव
दावियेला देही ।
मी तू पण गेले
ठायीच्या ठायी ॥४॥

Chokha says solace
Of my mind he is
Hence I sing praise
Of Namdev

चोखा म्हणे माझा
जीवीचा विसावा ।
पोकरितो धावा
नामदेवा ॥५॥

ଓଓଓ || **78** || ଌଌଌ

So debased caste
Body too impure
Not knowing pure
Unadulterated

Still, he bestowed
His grace upon me
Destroyed ignorance
Muddled up

Great condemnation
From great many
All of it ineffective
By his grace

Therefore, my mind
Welded to his feet
Chokha says further
What to speak

•~•

बहू हीन याति
देह अमंगळ ।
न कळे चोखाळ
चोखट ते ॥१॥

परी इही केले
मज कृपादान ।
निरसिले अज्ञान
मळकट ॥२॥

बहुता परीचा
बहुताचा बोल ।
तो झाला फोल
कृपादृष्टी ॥३॥

म्हणोनि जीवे
धरियेले पाय ।
चोखा म्हणे काय
बोलू आता ॥४॥

•~•

ଓଓଓ || **79** || ଌଌଌ

What marketplace? Whose sack?
Distinct always is the Owner

Goods belong to whom? Who is the seller?
All the transactions remain undisclosed

On the sun setting, closes the marketplace
All hustle and bustle go away

Chokha says the measure is brimming to top
In whose hands should I empty it?

•~•

कैसा हा हाट कवणाची गोणी ।
वेगळाचि राहिला मालधणी ॥१॥

कवणाचा वाण विकितसे कवण ।
अवघा पसारा ठेवी झाकोन ॥२॥

मावळला दिन झाकलासे हाट ।
अवघा वारलासे बोभाट ॥३॥

चोखा म्हणे माप भरियेले सिगे ।
आता कोणाचे पदरी देऊ उगे ॥४॥

•~•

☙☙☙ || 80 || ❧❧❧

Whose companionship
To seek? For whom?
Nothing but sorrows
Engulfing thence

Hence Namdev's
Feet I have held
On remembering them
Contentment

Bliss of bliss
He showed me
Joy incarnate
On the brick

Chokha says life
Namdev is mine
Prostrate I lie
In front of him

कोणाचा संग
धरू कोणासाठी ।
तो दुःखाचीच मिठी
पडे तेणे ॥१॥

म्हणोनी नामयाचे
धरियेले पाय ।
आठविता होय
समाधान ॥२॥

सुखाचे सुख
मज दावियेले डोळा ।
आनंद सावळा
विटेवरी ॥३॥

चोखा म्हणे माझा
नामदेव प्राण ।
घालीन लोटांगण
जीवे भावे ॥४॥

ぐぐぐ || **81** || ぶぶぶ

Bliss unparalleled
At the feet of the saint
In person at Alandi
He resides

He is my lord
Dnyaneshwar Mauli[1]
Who uncovered the essence
Of the Upanishadas[2]

For the sake of
The upliftment
Of all the downtrodden
And the desire-bound

Chokha says glorious
The treatise, *Dnyandevi*
On reading it, the beings
Find the Lord

●৩৩●

सुख अनुपम
संतांचे चरणीं ।
प्रत्यक्ष अलंकाभुवनी
नांदतसे ॥१॥

तो हा महाराज
ज्ञानेश्वर माउली ।
जेणे निगमवल्ली
प्रगट केली ॥२॥

संसारी आसक्त
माया मोहे रत ।
ऐसे जे पतित
तारावया ॥३॥

चोखा म्हणे श्रेष्ठ
ज्ञानदेवी ग्रंथ ।
वाचिता सनाथ
जीव होती ॥४॥

●৩৩●

1 Mauli (माउली) means mother. This is the title that the Varkari tradition has lovingly bestowed upon Sant Dnyandev, aka Dnyaneshwar, for his contribution in giving the contemporary society a new direction.

2 Here, the Poet refers to Dnyandev's seminal work, *Dnyaneshwari* or *Dnyandevi*, a groundbreaking commentary upon *Bhagvad Gita*. *Dnyaneshwari* provides the ethical/philosophical foundation to the Varkari Sect.

||| 82 |||

You are my Mother You are my Mother You are my Mother O Vitthal	माझी तू माउली माझी तू माऊली । माझी तू माउली विठ्ठल तू ॥१॥
Why did you forsake me? Why separated me from You? Why did You send me To Mangalvedha[1]?	मज का मोकलिले वेगळे का केले । का बा धाडियेले मंगळवेढ्या ॥२॥
Had I become such A burden for You That You distanced me From Your feet?	काय माझा भार झालासे जोजार । म्हणोनी केले दूर पायांपरते ॥३॥
Chokha says I do not Care for the wages When I can sing sweet Praise of Yours	चोखा म्हणे मज द्रव्याची नाही चाड । तुझे नाम गोड मुखी गाता ॥४॥

1 A town not far from Pandarpur where the Poet was taken to work on the construction of town-wall. Unfortunately, the wall collapsed killing many of the labourers, including the Poet. This poem and the next were composed during his stay at Mangalvedha.

|| 83 ||

All that I desire
Is to behold Your feet
There is nothing else
I long for

Bestow upon me
Your grace ever
And blissful stay
Next to Namdev's

Give me place
At Your door
This is all, O Lord
I ask of You

Chokha says today
I feel dejected
Moment to moment
Longing for Pandhari

राहिली वासना
पायांसवे चाड ।
आन नाही कोड
माझे काही ॥१॥

तुमची कृपादृष्टी
असावी मजवरी ।
आणि नामया सेजारी
सुखवस्ती ॥२॥

महाद्वारापुढे
मज ठाव द्यावा ।
हेचि केशवा
मागतसे ॥३॥

चोखा म्हणे आजि
वाटते उदास ।
घडिये घडिये आस
पंढरीची ॥४॥

ଔଔଔ || 84 || ഋഋഋ

Mine own have become Strangers for me It amazes me Amusingly	माझे मज हे झालेसे पारखे । नवल कवतुके मज वाटे ॥१॥
I toiled day and night For all of them Mine own have turned Their backs on me	होऊनि काबाडी वागविले सारे । माझे मजवर फिरलेसे ॥२॥
Good-bad, my own morsels I fed in their mouths I nourished their beings For their happiness	वोखटे गोमटे तोंडीचे घातिले । पिंड हे पोसिले सुखासाठी ॥३॥
Chokha says I became All alone, all alone All ran away Seeing hardships	चोखा म्हणे झालो एकटा एकला । पळाली अवकळा देखोनिया ॥४॥

൞൞൞ || 85 || ൞൞൞

Abandoning those in Your refuge
What are you going to gain?
Scriptures narrate ancient tales
All of them in vain

Rejecting those in Your refuge
That will be such a shame
I will proclaim this to all
Know this my resolve

Why is that motto[1] tied at Your feet?
Just throw, throw it away, O Lord
Tall tales of Your benevolence
No one to rescue me

Chokha says You are omniscient
Vedas know not Your pre-eminence
Upanishads too admit ignorance
What me wretched is to say

शरणांगता मोकलिता ।
काय येईल तुमचे हाता ।
पुराणे सांगती जुनाट कथा ।
ते सर्व अप्राप्त ॥१॥

शरणांगताचा अव्हेर ।
करिता बोल लागेल फार ।
ऐसा माझा निर्धार ।
डांगोरा पिटीन ॥२॥

ब्रीद का बांधिले चरणीं ।
ते सोडी सोडी चक्रपाणी ।
वायाचि झालीसे कहाणी ।
कोण निर्वाणी सोडी मज ॥३॥

चोखा म्हणे तुम्ही सुजाण ।
वेदा न कळे महिमान ।
श्रुति शीणती नेति नेति म्हणोन ।
तेथे मी दीन काय वानू ॥४॥

1 Lord Vitthal wears anklets which have inscriptions, declaring the Lord to be the Protector of His worshippers.

|| 86 ||

You brought me up
You nurtured me
You alone showed
This world to me

Your ways and means
You alone know
We very well know
Our own cause

What is it, O Lord
That makes You hesitate?
Pray, tell me, O Lord
But only this

Chokha says what more
Should I speak?
You are my Saviour
O Lord of the lords

तुम्ही वाढविले
तुम्ही पोशियेले ।
तुम्हीच दाविले
जग मज ॥१॥

तुमचा प्रकार
तुमचा तुम्ही जाणा ।
आमुचिया खुणा
जाणो आम्ही ॥१॥

तुम्हासी तो भीड
कासयाची देवा ।
हेचि बा केशवा
सांगा मज ॥३॥

चोखा म्हणे काय
बोलू ययावरी ।
माझा तू कैवारी
देवराया ॥४॥

|| 87 ||

Just once rid me, O Lord Of this burning anguish Then I will not ever Grumble again	एक वेळा करी शीतळ तळमळ । मग मी मळमळ न करी काही ॥१॥
Remembering Your feet Will remain satisfied That bliss in heart I will cherish	चिंतोनिया पाय राहिन धणीवरी । सुख ते अंतरी साठवीन ॥२॥
Attachments and desires I have relinquished I bank upon You Every which way	लाग या लोभाचा न धरी आधार । घालीन सर्व भार तुजवरी ॥३॥
Chokha says now Relieve me from this maze This riddle of life Frightening, O Lord	चोखा म्हणे आता वारा हे साकडे । भवाचे ते कोडे भय देवा ॥४॥

ଔଔଔ || 88 || ଌଌଌ

Now no more at all
Fascination for these
Disgust I am filled with
For the worldly matters

आता याचा छंद
नकोसा हा झाला ।
वोकुठा आला
संसाराचा ॥१॥

Food gone bad
How repulses one
Same happens to me
Regarding this

विटले जे अन्न
घेतसे चिळशी ।
तैसे ये विषयी
झाले असे ॥२॥

Now all of these
Sources of miseries
I cannot bear
Patiently anymore

आता हे अवघे
दुःखाचे प्रकार ।
न सोसवे धीर
धरवेना ॥३॥

Chokha says enough
Of these worldly matters
They take me away
From the Supreme Gain

चोखा म्हणे आता
पुरे याचे जिणे ।
पुढील ते पेणे
अंतरले ॥४॥

|| 89 ||

Pollution for Vedas
Pollution for Shastras
Puranas[1] are filled with
Demeaning pollution

Pollution for the being
Pollution for the Beyond
Body is filled with
Demeaning pollution

Pollution for Brahma
Pollution for Vishnu
Pollution for Shankar
Demeaning

Pollution in the birth
Pollution in the death
Chokha says pollution
Origin to End

वेदासी विटाळ
शास्त्रासी विटाळ ।
पुराणे अमंगळ
विटाळाची ॥१॥

जीवासी विटाळ
शिवासी विटाळ ।
काया अमंगळ
विटाळाची ॥२॥

ब्रह्मीया विटाळ
विष्णूसी विटाळ ।
शंकरा विटाळ
अमंगळ ॥३॥

जन्मता विटाळ
मरता विटाळ ।
चोखा म्हणे विटाळ
आदिअंती ॥४॥

1 Ancient Indian religious texts that consist mainly of mythology.

ঌঌঌ || **90** || ঌঌঌ

I have made this
Resolve in my mind
Your tempting, O Lord
Enough now

My burdens on You
Heaped I have all
This I know myself
Well indeed

Speaking trifles
Seems worthless
I do not have much
Strength in me

Chokha says happily
I will sit protesting
That will only dent
Your eminence

•~•

माझा मी विचार
केला असे मना ।
चाळवण नारायणा
पुरे तुमचे ॥१॥

तुम्हांवरी भार
घातिलेसे वोझे ।
हेचि मी माझे
जाणतसे ॥२॥

वाउगे बोलावे
दिसे फलकट ।
नाही बळकट
वर्म आंगी ॥३॥

चोखा म्हणे सुखे
बैसेन धरणा ।
तुमच्या थोरपणा
येईल लाज ॥४॥

•~•

ଓଓଓ || **91** || ଛଛଛ

Not bothering whether
It seems good or bad
I will proclaim the truth
Far and wide, O Lord

जगामध्ये दिसे
बरे की वाईट।
ऐसाचि बोभाट
करीन देवा ॥१॥

Now how long
Should I hesitate?
You apparently
Know it well

आता कोठवरी
धरावी हे भीड ।
तुम्ही तो उघड
जाणतसा ॥२॥

"The Protector" motto
Flaunts on Your anklet
Reputed in Three Worlds
You are such

ब्रीदाचा तोडर
बांधलासे पायी ।
त्रिभुवनी ग्वाही
तुमची आहे ॥३॥

Chokha says whatever
That harms not Your glory
Undertake such a course
Better, O Lord

चोखा म्हणे जेणे
न ये उणेपण ।
तेचि ते कारण
जाणा देवा ॥४॥

ഗ്ഗ || **92** || ഇഇഇ

Ceremonial thread adorning waist
That is the goldsmith Narhari[1]

Tinklets on feet chime sweetly
That is the dearest Namdev

Anklet on the left foot
Sounds prominently Parisa[2]

Anklet on the right foot
Sings aloud the songs of Jaidev[3]

The beautiful feet on the brick
That is, know well, Chokha Mela

करी सूत्र शोभे कटावरी ।
तोचि हा सोनार नरहरी ॥१॥

पायीं वाजती रुणझुण घंटा ।
तोचि नामयाचा नागर विठा ॥२॥

वाम चरणीचा तोडरू ।
परिसा उठतसे डीगरू ॥३॥

दक्षिण चरणीचा तोडरू ।
जयदेव पदाचा गजरू ॥४॥

विटेवरी चरण कमळा ।
तो हा जाणा चोखा मेळा ॥५॥

1 A Varkari Saint, the Poet's contemporary
2 A Varkari Saint, the Poet's contemporary
3 A 12th century devotional poet, well-known for his Geet Govinda

|| 93 ||

Love infinite
Namdev obtained
That we received
For eternity

आवडीचे प्रेम
नामया लाधले ।
ते आम्हा फावले
जन्मोजन्मी ॥१॥

Therefore, in Pandhari
On the banks of Bhima
Where the Lord on the brick
Hands on hips

म्हणोनी पंढरी
विटेवरी हरी ।
भिवरेचे तिरी
कर कटी ॥२॥

Sins extraordinaire
Are absolved at sight
Such is the boon
Granted to Pundalik

महा पातकियासी
दरुशने उद्धार ।
ऐसा दिला वर
पुंडलिका ॥३॥

For twenty-eight eons
Has not sat down
With joined feet
Still standing

अठ्ठावीस युगे
न बैसे खाली ।
समचि पाउली
उभा असे ॥४॥

Chokha says such is
The Protector of devotees
Compassionate towards
The faithful

चोखा म्हणे ऐसा
भक्तांचा आळुका ।
कनवाळु देखा
भाविकांचा ॥५॥

|| **94** ||

Somewhere one
Somewhere two
But in Pandhari
The Absolute

Somewhere deity
Somewhere holy water
But in Pandhari
Everything

Somewhere thrones
Somewhere robes
But in Pandhari
Feet on the brick

Somewhere sleeping
Somewhere sitting
But in Pandhari
Always standing

Chokha says
Whatever wherever
But in Pandhari
With open arms

कोठे एक
कोठे दोन ।
आहे परिपूर्ण
पंढरीये ॥१॥

कोठे देव
कोठे तीर्थ ।
आहे सर्व
पंढरीये ॥२॥

कोठे आसन
कोठे वसन ।
विटे समचरण
पंढरीये ॥३॥

कोठे निजे
कोठे बैसे ।
उभाचि असे
पंढरीये ॥४॥

चोखा म्हणे
कोठे काही ।
उभारूनी बाही
पंढरीये ॥५॥

ॳॳॳ || **95** || ॳॳॳ

The Lord is standing	देव हा उभा
The Lord is standing	देव हा उभा ।
The Lord is standing	देव हा उभा
On the brick	विटेवरी ॥१॥
Within all beings	सर्वां ठायी
The Lord is standing	देव उभा ।
Beauty of the Cosmos	त्रैलोक्य शोभा
In Pandhari	पंढरीये ॥२॥
Pray, behold the Lord	देव पाहा कोणी
Pray, behold the Lord	देव पाहा कोणी ।
Standing with joined feet	उभा समचरणीं
On the brick	विटेवरी ॥३॥
Chokha says ours	चोखा म्हणे
Blissful trove of bliss	सुखाची सुखराशी ।
Our patrimony	आमुची मिराशी
In Pandhari	पंढरीये ॥४॥

ঙঙঙ || 96 || ঌঌঌ

Sufferings of eternity
Who else will rid of?
Persecuted in this world
Rescue me, O Lord

I surrender at Your feet
O Lord of the Yadavas
Allaying all my fears
Help me cross this ocean

Without You who will
Take me out of this maze?
I have become insane
I see no solution

Chokha says, O Lord Almighty
Now allay this anguish of life
I rest my head, O Vitthal
On Your feet

●~●

जन्मांची वेरझारी ।
तुम्हांविण कोण वारी ।
जाचलो संसारी ।
सोडवण करी देवराया ॥१॥

शरण शरण पंढरीराया ।
तुम्हा आलो यादवराया ।
निवारोनिया भया ।
मज तारा या सागरी ॥२॥

तुम्हांविण माझे कोडे ।
कोण निवारी साकडे ।
मी तो झालो असे वेडे ।
उपाव पुढे सुचेना ॥३॥

चोखा म्हणे दीनानाथा ।
आता निवारी हे भवव्यथा ।
म्हणोनी ठेवितसे माथा ।
चरणावरी विठूच्या ॥४॥

●~●

ఆఆఆ || 97 || ఌఌఌ

Showing mercy
Protect me, O Lord

I am wretched, wretched
Surrendered at Your feet

Such a shame it will be for You
On abandoning me, O Lord

Preserve Your reputation
Promising me shelter

Chokha says, O Lord
Now hesitate not at all

●〜●

करोनिया दया ।
सांभाळाजी देवराया ॥१॥

मी तो पतित पतित ।
तुमचाचि शरणांगत ॥२॥

लाज येईल तुमचे नावा ।
मज उपेक्षिता देवा ॥३॥

आपुले जतन ।
करा अभय देवोन ॥४॥

चोखा म्हणे हरि ।
आता भीड न धरी ॥५॥

●〜●

|| 98 ||

Anxious my mind
Rambles helter-skelter
Rescue me from this
O Lord of the lords

I have become restless
What should I do now?
Not able to restrain
The unrestrained

This racket is Yours
You better get rid of it
Please take us out
Of all this

Chokha says then alone
My mind will find bliss
Enough of the sorrows
Henceforth, O Lord

बावरले मन
करी धावाधावी ।
यांतुनी सोडवी
देवराया ॥१॥

लागलासे चाळा
काय करू आता ।
नावरे वारिता
अनावर ॥२॥

तुमचे लिगाड
तुम्हीच वारावे ।
आम्हासी काढावे
यातोनिया ॥३॥

चोखा म्हणे तरीच
जीवा होय सुख ।
नका आता दुःख
दाऊ देवा ॥४॥

ඏඏඏ || **99** || ෴෴෴

How my mind Longs for it! Does not wish for Anything else	वेध हा कैसा लागला वो जीवा । नाठवेचि हेवा दुजा काही ॥१॥
En route to Pandhari Arrive Varkaris Talking to them Is such a bliss	पंढरीचे वाटे येती वारकरी । सुखाची मी करी मात तया ॥२॥
Those who sing Praise of my Vitthal My source of bliss Those Varkaris	माझ्या विठोबाचे गाती जे नाम । ते माझे सुखधाम वारकरी ॥३॥
Having arrived, I will Prostrate in front of them Happily, I will take them In my arms	लोटांगणे सामोरा जाईन तयांसी । क्षेम आनंदेसी देईन त्यासी ॥४॥
Chokha says they are Life of my life I will receive them With utmost devotion	चोखा म्हणे माझा प्राणाचा तो प्राण । जाईन वोवाळोन जीवे भावे ॥५॥

෴ || 100 || ෴

Salutation, o my parents, salutation[1]
I am Mahar of Your Mahar

Have got exceedingly hungry
Have come for Your leftovers[2]

Have come with great hopes
I am servant of Your servant

Chokha says this basket
Have brought for Your leftovers

जोहार मायबाप जोहार ।
तुमच्या महाराचा मी महार ॥१॥

बहु भुकेला जाहलो ।
तुमच्या उष्ट्यासाठी आलो ॥२॥

बहु केली आस ।
तुमच्या दासाचा मी दास ॥३॥

चोखा म्हणे पाटी ।
आणिली तुमच्या उष्ट्यासाठी ॥४॥

1 Being placed at the bottom of the caste hierarchy, it was mandatory for all the 'outcastes' to greet the so-called upper caste people with reverence by bending as low as possible, head almost touching the ground.

2 The members of the Mahar community had to beg for their livelihood, despite performing all their laborious duties. At the end of the day, they would go from door to door shouting salutations (*johaar* in Marathi) for the master and the lady of the house, carrying a bamboo basket to collect the stale food that would be dropped from a distance in that basket.

APPENDIX

A distinct feature of all major Varkari Saint-poets is that a large number of 'satellite poets' also composed poems under their influence. Chokha Mela also has his satellite poets in his family members - Soyara, his wife; Nirmala, his sister; Karma Mela, his son; and Banka, Nirmala's husband. Each of these are great poets on their own and also provide important biographical details about Chokha Mela. What caliber these four have, one can get a fair idea from these specimen poems.

SOYARA

All colours One became
In colours is coloured the Colour Supreme

Selfhood has gone to waste
On seeing the Lord of Pandhari

No place for discrimination
Ran away the anger, the lust

Despite being, you are Beyond
Ever in Samadhi, behold

Beholder, beholding have vanished
Says Chokha's Mahari[1]

अवघा रंग एक झाला ।
रंगी रंगला श्रीरंग ॥१॥

मी तूपण गेले वाया ।
पाहता पंढरीच्या राया ॥२॥

नाही भेदाचे ते काम ।
पळोनी गेले क्रोध काम ॥३॥

देही असुनी विदेही ।
सदा समाधिस्थ पाही ॥४॥

पाहते पाहणे गेले दुरी ।
म्हणे चोखयाची महारी ॥५॥

1 This is how Soyara addresses herself in her poems, a unique signature style indeed! She is perhaps the first person to appropriate a term that was supposed to be an insult (a very postmodern phenomenon) and goes on, instead, to flaunt it proudly in all her poems!

NIRMALA

All this while	आजिवरी तुम्ही
You protected him	तयासी पाळिले ।
Forgiving Chokha	अपराध साहिले
All his offences	चोखियाचे ॥१॥
After he is gone	तयाचिया पाठी
Are You tired of us?	आमुचा कंटाळा ।
Please tell me this	आला का दयाळा
O Lord	सांगा मज ॥२॥
Debased, wretched me	हीनदीन मी
Committed endless sins	पातकांची राशी ।
I surrender at Your feet	शरण पायांसी
With all my being	जीवे भावे ॥३॥
Nirmala says, O Lord	निर्मळा म्हणे
You are compassionate	तुम्ही तो दयाळ ।
Hence protect me	म्हणोनी सांभाळ
As Your own	करा माझा ॥४॥

BANKA

The lord of the learned	ज्ञानियांचा राजा
Dnyaneshwar Mauli	ज्ञानेश्वर माउली ।
Showered his grace	खेचरा वोळली
On Khechar[1]	कृपासिंधु ॥१॥
On Dnyandev's feet	ज्ञानदेवा चरणीं
Surrendered Khechar	खेचर शरण ।
Who graced Namdev	नामदेवा पूर्ण
Absolutely	कृपा केली ॥२॥
Namdev placed his hand	नामदेवे हात
On Chokha's head	चोखियाचे शिरी ।
Blessed him by teaching	विठ्ठल तीं अक्षरी
Three syllables, Vitthala	उपदेशिले ॥३॥
Banka says mine	बंका म्हणे माझा
Chokha is Guru	चोखा गुरु माउली ।
I lie prostrate	तयाचे पाउलीं
At his feet	लोटांगण ॥४॥

1 Visoba Khechar was a Brahmin of Alandi village who incessantly persecuted Dnyandev and his siblings initially, only to become one of their most ardent followers. He happens to be Sant Namdev's Guru.

Chokha pure, unadulterated
No stain at all in his being

Chokha is the ocean of bliss
Chokha is the field of devotion

Chokha is mother affectionate
Chokha is the shelter of grace

Chokha is the solace of my mind
Banka lies prostrate in front of him

चोखा चोखट निर्मळ ।
तया अंगी नाही मळ ॥१॥

चोखा सुखाचा सागर ।
चोखा भक्तीचा आगर ॥२॥

चोखा प्रेमाची माउली ।
चोखा कृपेची साउली ॥३॥

चोखा मनाचे मोहन ।
बंका घाली लोटांगण ॥४॥

KARMA MELA

You created our caste the basest
Why don't You understand, O Lord?

Whole life spent eating leftovers
You don't feel ashamed of it

At our home, curd and rice
You ate, how can you deny?

Says Chokha's Karma Mela
Why did You give me birth?

आमुची केली हीन याती ।
तुज का न कळे श्रीपती ॥१॥

जन्म गेला उष्टे खाता ।
लाज न ये तुमचे चित्ता ॥२॥

आमुचे घरी भात दही ।
खावोनी कैसा म्हणसी नाही ॥३॥

म्हणे चोखियाचा कर्ममेळा ।
कासया जन्म दिला मला ॥४॥

Our father's savings
Why don't You return it to us?

How is this conduct of Yours?
Pleading, I have exhausted, O Lord

How many times to and fro
Meaninglessly, should I go?

Karma Mela says, O Lord
How long should I plead thus?

आमुच्या बापाचे ठेवणे ।
का तू न देसी आम्हा कारणे ॥१॥

कैसी तुझी नीत बरी ।
मागता शिणलो मी हरी ॥२॥

वाउग्या येरझारा ।
किती कराव्या दातारा ॥३॥

कर्ममेळा म्हणे हरी ।
किती मागावे निर्धारी ॥४॥

Alphabetical List of the First Lines of the Poems

****

वर्णानुक्रमे अभंगांच्या पहिल्या ओळी

****

Sitaram Mhatre Foundation's Other Publication

THE AUTOBIOGRAPHY OF SANT BAHINABAI

Sant Bahinabai (1628-1700) was just three years old when she was married off to a 30-year-old widower. Here starts a long series of hardships that Bahinabai had to brave out for the better part of her life. Hardly had she turned seven, when she had to leave their native place along with her family and go in search of livelihood from village to village and town to town, and that too on foot. No one knew when or where the next meal would be. To worsen the matters, Bahinabai's short tempered husband accompanied her family during these seemingly endless journeys and Bahinabai was subjected to the most brutal form of domestic violence at the hands of her husband from a very tender age (even when she was three months pregnant). This travesty of a married life continued for almost a decade and her birth in the so-called higher caste did next to nothing to alleviate Bahinabai's misery, just like millions of women before and after her. What makes Bahinabai's sufferings significant is the fact that she gave them a voice in her poems and became the first woman autobiographer of India. Her autobiography ranks very high among those works that document the lives of survivors of domestic violence, apart from being one of the oldest, if not THE oldest, such an account in the history of world literature. With its uninhibited attacks on patriarchy, Bahinabai's autobiography predates all the feminist texts in the world. This book also contains Bahinabai's translation of Vajrasuchi Upanishad, which makes her the first woman translator of India.

www.ingramcontent.com/pod-product-compliance
Lightning Source LLC
LaVergne TN
LVHW101923220826
846093LV00009B/349

* 9 7 8 8 1 9 6 0 9 1 1 7 0 *